Leading the Learner-Centered Campus

Michael Harris
Roxanne Cullen

Leading the Learner-Centered Campus

An Administrator's Framework for Improving Student Learning Outcomes

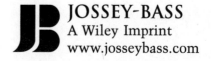

JOSSEY-BASS
A Wiley Imprint
www.josseybass.com

Library of Congress Cataloging-in-Publication Data

Harris, Michael, 1956-
  Leading the learner-centered campus : an administrator's framework for improving student learning outcomes / Michael Harris, Roxanne Cullen.
     p. cm. – (The Jossey-Bass higher and adult education series)
  Includes bibliographical references and index.
  ISBN 978-0-470-40298-6 (cloth)
  1. Universities and colleges–Administration. 2. School improvement programs.
3. Educational change. I. Cullen, Roxanne Mann. II. Title.
  LB2341.H324 2010
  378.1'01–dc22

                                                                    2010003735

Printed in the United States of America

FIRST EDITION

HB Printing 10 9 8 7 6 5 4 3 2 1

The Jossey-Bass Higher and
Adult Education Series

Contents

Foreword

Interest in the learned-centered paradigm, largely launched by Barr and Tagg's now widely referenced 1995 *Change* magazine article, remains high. Unlike many other new ideas with fleeting popularity, this one continues to generate dialogue, both among faculty in the classroom and among academic leaders who envision institutions more focused on learning.

The idea that students should be more responsible for learning and that teaching should be about facilitating that learning has resonated with faculty who deal with students who are, now more than ever, passive and reliant on teachers to direct every aspect of their learning. Not only do the ideas of learner-centered teaching make sense theoretically, college teachers across disciplines have successfully implemented instructional approaches that reflect this new focus on learning. The pedagogical literature of the disciplines is replete with examples of group-work assignments, service learning opportunities, collaborative testing structures, and online discussion forums that illustrate how teachers are encouraging students to see themselves as learners who are responsible for what and how they learn. Across the board, faculty report, and in many cases document, that these approaches positively impact student motivation and result in deeper learning experiences.

So far, learner-centered teaching has mostly been a grassroots movement, changing the landscape of higher education classroom by classroom. The progress is slow, and resistance from students and faculty is common. That students resist is expected; these approaches require that students do more of the tasks associated with learning. For instance, the teacher may ask them to generate examples, rather than copying down examples the teacher lists in class.

That faculty resist and challenge the veracity of pedagogies more focused on learning and less centered on teaching is more perplexing. In part, this resistance derives from not knowing how to teach in these ways, but it also bespeaks a lack of institutional commitment to the learner-centered paradigm. Academic leaders often pay lip service to the idea of becoming a learner-centered institution, but few colleges and universities have put any institutional muscle behind the move to become learner-centered. Creating a climate for learning in a classroom is not accomplished by decree, just as creating a learner-centered institution is not accomplished with public relations materials that proclaim its presence.

Perhaps institutions can be partly excused because higher education has only recently—and incompletely—considered what makes an institution learner-centered. It's fine to say that your institution is learner-centered, and it's probably even necessary to regularly reiterate that commitment. However, creating a learner-centered college or university takes leadership at every level and a clear understanding of what policies, practices, procedures, and priorities make learning the energy-center of the institution. What precisely and specifically that entails brings us to the need for and value of this book.

Right from the start, those writing about learner-centered teaching and learning-centered institutions have noted that this kind of change requires a paradigm shift in thinking about institutional goals and priorities. Unfortunately, "paradigm shift" has become something of a cliché used to describe almost any kind of realignment. In this book, Harris and Cullen point out that the kind of change they write about requires something much more dramatic than moving from one line to another and is not a seamless transition. The opening chapters of this book ably elaborate on the significant changes involved when an institution makes a commitment to become learning-centered.

The power of the authors' voices derives from experience. Yes, they know the literature, amply referencing and documenting the theory and research behind the learning-centered paradigm, but they have also lived what they write about. Their institutional context is similar to what most of us experience. Theirs is not an elitist institution with selective enrollment and a large endowment; it's a frontline institution with needy students and inadequate resources. The relevance of the authors' experience adds legitimacy and power to how they propose to realize the goals of the learner-centered paradigm. If becoming learning-centered can happen at institutions like theirs, it can happen anywhere.

Harris and Cullen also write with understanding of and appreciation for grassroots leadership. If classrooms are to become learner-centered, faculty need the local support of their departments. Professors working to implement learner-centered approaches need access to material resources and faculty development opportunities. They need to be working in an environment that values collaboration and recognizes how much faculty can learn from and with each other. They need department and division chairs who recognize that efforts to implement instructional changes don't always go smoothly, and that sometimes students complain to local leaders about the learning experiences they most need to have ("That professor made us do all the work!"). Harris and Cullen offer department chairs and other local leaders a plethora of information, ideas, and advice that can directly support efforts at the departmental level to become more learning-centered.

Chapter Seven, for example, tackles the tough issue of faculty evaluation and makes clear the important distinction between formative and summative evaluation. Academic leaders need one kind of information to make personnel decisions; faculty need very different kinds of information to implement changes that positively impact learning outcomes. Moreover, if the goal is to use pedagogies that engage and involve students, then the instruments used to assess instruction should not be asking numerous questions about didactic teaching methods. It's a chapter that beautifully illustrates how efforts to become learner-centered involve changes that depend on leadership at every level within the institution.

As Chapter Eight points out, the configuration of learning spaces, like classrooms, can become symbols of a new commitment to learning. Classrooms with seats permanently laid out in rows with a podium positioned in front do not encourage faculty to use group work. Classrooms with moveable seats and a less clearly defined front of the room make students and teachers aware of the possibilities of learning together.

You'll enjoy reading this book. Harris and Cullen offer material that is intellectually rich and provocative yet, at the same time, pragmatic and useful. How these authors propose making institutions learner-centered is rooted in reality. What they propose is sensible and doable. For any academic leader, whether a faculty curriculum committee chair, a department head, dean, provost, president, or the person charged with orienting new faculty, this book offers much needed wisdom on those realities that make institutions learning-centered.

Maryellen Weimer

We would like to dedicate this book to our families for the sacrifices they have made. For their support, understanding, encouragement, love, and patience.

Michael Harris dedicates this book to his wife, Tali, and his sons, Ronen, Asaf, and Amit.

Roxanne Cullen dedicates this book to her husband, John Cullen.

Preface

Institutional core values, unlike missions, are intended to represent the values that underlie our work, our interactions, our practices. They guide our decision making, direct our processes, determine how we reward accomplishments, and represent our most fundamental beliefs. They are the values of the paradigm in which we operate.

In 2004, the authors of *The Future of Higher Education: Rhetoric Reality and the Risks of the Market*, an investigation of the market forces affecting higher education, wrote, "[T]he list of . . . fissures between higher education's rhetoric and its performance is long and it is growing" (Newman, Couturier, & Scurry, p. 6). One of those fissures is the disconnect between institutionally espoused core values and practiced core values. The core values currently espoused by institutions of higher education on websites and in public documents reflect media trends and read like responses to the public concerns over a perceived lack of accountability. These statements more often represent rhetorical exercises in public relations rather than thorough, critical examinations of true operating values and processes.

In this book we argue that the disconnect between institutionally espoused values and true operating values is not solely a result of outside forces affecting institutions but rather the result of the anachronistic paradigm that dominates our thinking. Because of our unwitting acceptance of this paradigm, we operate according to a set of core values that we would not privately adhere to or publicly promote. Institutional rhetoric remains disconnected from the reality of institutional behaviors because of this phenomenon. What is needed is a shift from the instructional paradigm to the learner-centered paradigm.

Shifting Paradigms

The term *paradigm shift*, as originally used by Thomas Kuhn in *The Structure of Scientific Revolutions* (1962), referred exclusively to scientific theory; however, its meaning has become more generic and now refers to radical changes in thought that require complete reenvisioning of systems or organizations. To us, the word *shift* makes the challenge of radical change seem too easy, like changing place with someone in line or shifting gears on a bicycle, suggesting that if leadership makes one adjustment, the rest of the gears will fall into place and the new paradigm will be operational. But that will certainly not be the case. Shifting gears on bicycles allows riders to maintain their cadence as the terrain becomes more difficult. This is most definitely *not* how shifting paradigms works. Our cadences will be interrupted. Shifting paradigms is unbalancing and unsettling because it is about shifting thinking and attitudes.

Leading the transition to a learner-centered campus will involve everyone—governing boards, presidents, provosts, vice presidents, deans, chairs, faculty, academic and nonacademic staff, and, of course, students—reenvisioning their work. Shifting thinking and attitudes is an organizational metamorphosis requiring all parties to shed the old while growing the new. The shift that must take place is counterintuitive in many ways, thus requiring individuals to pay conscious attention to their actions and decisions.

Institutions of higher education are being challenged on all fronts, attempting to change their ways of doing business in order to answer calls for accountability, transparency, access, and relevancy. Incremental changes in response to these challenges abound; however, incremental changes are not enough. In order to respond to our rapidly changing environment, we need comprehensive change, a change in paradigms. The concept of shifting toward a learner-centered paradigm is certainly not new. Faculty in the United States and abroad have been experimenting and adopting learner-centered practices with great success. However, if the comprehensive shift to a new paradigm is to become a reality, then the efforts to transform our practices need to extend beyond the classroom. Institutions themselves must become realigned with the new paradigm to become learner-centered institutions.

Until now, little discussion has taken place regarding the role of administrators at all levels within institutions and in all areas of the institution, not solely academic affairs, in fostering this institutional shift. If the shift toward learner-centeredness is to be realized as a true paradigm shift, that discussion must begin. It is time for administrators to consider their role in making the paradigm shift a reality.

Purpose

The purpose of this book is to begin that discussion and to offer a method for campus leaders who are willing to take on the challenge of reenvisioning their own practices in order to make the shift in paradigms complete. Our aim is to provide leaders with a framework for examining their work in light of the instructional and learner-centered paradigms and to offer some specific strategies for critically examining habitual practices in order to make every aspect of our work intentional. The goal of this process is to bridge the disconnect between institutionally espoused values and our true operating values.

Audience

We offer leaders a method for change that recommends (1) examining their current practices to see how they are governed by the instructional paradigm; (2) considering how they could realign these practices to be consistent with the learner-centered paradigm; (3) finding ways to infuse assessment into the process to drive the change; and (4) modeling the way by adopting new behaviors that illustrate learner-centeredness within their own work habits. This process is one that leaders can apply to all facets of organizational behaviors or practices within their spheres of influence.

Department chairs can use this process to look at departmental procedures, such as scheduling classes, providing faculty development opportunities, or recruiting new faculty. Deans can apply the same process to college-wide systems and procedures, such as looking at the process for allocating budgets, developing and supporting new programming, procuring funds for needed equipment and learning spaces, or allocating faculty rewards and initiatives. Vice presidents, provosts, and presidents can follow the same process to analyze operating behaviors at the divisional or institutional levels.

Scope

In this book, we will provide an examination of the need to shift, offering an explanation for why change within institutions of higher education seems to be so difficult to achieve. We will frame that discussion in terms of the paradigm that currently governs our thinking and approach to problem solving, the instructional paradigm. There is a tremendous amount of personal challenge in this process for it asks us to step outside our habitual ways of doing things and to consider if time-honored practices that seem natural and logical to us are as natural and logical as we have assumed. The difficulty of recognizing our paradigm is best articulated by Stephen Brookfield (1995) when he writes, "Paradigmatic assumptions are the hardest of all assumptions to uncover. They are the structuring assumptions we use to order the world into fundamental categories. Usually we don't even recognize them as assumptions, even after they've been pointed out to us. Instead we insist that they're objectively valid renderings of reality, the facts we know them to be true" (p. 2). However, we must learn to see the paradigm we work in if we are to change it.

Part of the challenge in this process is resisting the temptation to look for technical solutions. We will argue that our penchant for looking for ways to fix things, or "how to do it," is an outgrowth of the instructional paradigm. In writing about process frontiers, which he defines as new areas of activity or modifications for organizations, organizational change theorist Peter Vaill (1996) warned, "Institutional learning philosophy and practice have bred into many of us an obsession with 'how to do it.' This obsession amounts to a desire *not* to have a learning experience! We do not want to go through the creative process that process frontiers require. Rather, we want a protocol that takes the messiness and anxiety out of the process frontier. We want our learning to be targeted and efficient" (p. 136). We would like reading this book to be a learning experience, so rather than providing a one-size-fits-all solution or practice, we ask readers to reflect, analyze, and create new possibilities within their own frame of reference by applying a more general framework. Although we provide examples of some of our attempts to put into practice this model for change, we resist offering specific directions on "how to do it." Rather, we present ways of seeing and trying to train ourselves to see in a new way, to remove the corrective lens of the instructional paradigm.

Book Structure

The first four chapters, Part I, are organized around this conception of change. Chapter 1 presents the context for change, the forces affecting higher education that make the time conducive to action. Chapter 2 examines the reason for change, namely, the instructional paradigm that governs our current operations. We look at specific features of the paradigm: issues of power and control,

ownership of knowledge, organizational fragmentation, and isolation and unhealthy competition. Reviewers of our manuscript
accused us of adopting a "finger-wagging" attitude in this chapter,
as if we were anti-administration. If our fingers are indeed wagging, they are not wagging at administrators but at the paradigm
that makes administrative work so very difficult. We argue that it is
the attributes of the instructional paradigm that make change difficult to manage and likewise the factors that make administrative
work so demanding and in some cases unfulfilling. Chapter 3 examines the goal of change, the learner-centered paradigm. We begin
the chapter with an overview of the characteristics of the learner-
centered paradigm and the research on learning upon which it is
based, trying to make a case for why this knowledge is necessary for
academic leaders. Chapter 4 offers an examination of the leadership qualities that individuals must have in order to lead the shift to
the new paradigm. We review the literature on leadership according to three main features of the learner-centered paradigm: power
sharing, community building, and assessment and evaluation.

Lick (2002) notes that in order to shift paradigms, a new breed
of leader is required, one who is able to "lead the new paradigm from
rough concept to practical application" (p. 30). Part II provides the
practical applications. Chapter 5 looks at ways of fostering faculty
development in the new paradigm. Chapter 6 presents a framework for orienting new faculty based on the learning community
model. Chapter 7 considers the evaluation of teaching quality in the
new paradigm, and Chapter 8 looks at renovating physical learning
spaces to accommodate learner-centered practices. Each chapter in
Part II first considers how current practices are informed by the
instructional paradigm and then offers an illustration of how we
attempted to realign the practice within the framework of the new
paradigm, infusing assessment to drive the change and modeling
best practices in the process.

Acknowledgments

Many individuals have helped us during our research and writing. Two special individuals made this book possible. Thomas Ehrlich, Senior Scholar, The Carnegie Foundation, and Former President of Indiana University, and Anthony J. Diekema, Former President of Calvin College. Both are mentors to Michael. We also wish to make particular mention of Maryellen Weimer, who supported the concept and development of this manuscript from its inception; David Brightman, whose belief in the project and editorial expertise were of profound assistance; David's assistant, Aneesa Davenport; Cathy Mallon, who oversaw production; Paul Blake and Reinhold Hill, who read drafts and gave thoughtful commentary; Ariel Harris for his unconditional love and support; Roy Tamir for his friendship, support, and belief; Mindy Britton for her commitment and dedication; Ron Snead and George Menoutes, who serve as models of value-based ethical leadership; the Jossey-Bass reviewers for helpful comments; Judith DaDay, who assisted with editing; and Mary Ply, who coordinated scheduling and provided untold administrative support. Finally, we acknowledge and express gratitude to the many students, faculty, staff, and administrators whom we learned so much from and who helped us create the vision.

About the Authors

Michael Harris serves as the provost and vice president for Academic Affairs at Kettering University and as a professor of public policy. He received a Ph.D. in public policy from Indiana University, a master's degree from Tel-Aviv University, and an undergraduate degree in economics and business administration from Bar-Ilan University. He is a graduate of two of the Harvard Graduate School of Education's programs (IEM and MDP). He has published three books as well as articles in a variety of journals. Dr. Harris has been recognized for his teaching excellence and serves as a political commentator to a variety of broadcast and print media.

Roxanne Cullen is a professor of English at Ferris State University, where she has also served as Writing Center director, administrative head of the Department of Languages and Literature, interim associate dean of the College of Arts and Sciences, and assistant and associate vice president for Academic Affairs. In addition to her administrative service, she is a recipient of the university Distinguished Teaching Award. She received a Ph.D. in English from Bowling Green State University and a B.A. in English from SUNY Geneseo.

Leading the
Learner-Centered
Campus

Part I

Learner-Centered Leadership

While the focus on student learning has come to the forefront of institutional planning, there has been very little discussion of the magnitude of this proposed systemic change. Instead the focus has been on classroom pedagogy with most of the effort and literature on the learner-centered paradigm and the scholarship of teaching focused on strategies for faculty. And although incremental change has occurred, the larger, systemic change that defines a paradigm shift has not. The first four chapters that constitute Part I are about systemic change.

Lee Shulman, president of the Carnegie Foundation, noted how change occurs through critical reinterpretation: "Scholars develop powerful skeptical and critical capacities to reexamine old truths using the lenses of new conceptual frameworks" (Shulman, 2008, p. 7). A reinterpretation of old truths using a new lens is what we offer in Part I. While others have documented the market influences affecting higher education, the shortfalls of the current system, and the impact of demographic changes and offered solutions for various facets of this multifaceted challenge, we offer a systemic and sustainable solution by examining our core values in relation to the current paradigm and extend a framework for moving to a new paradigm. The focus in Part I is on the role of leadership in bringing about a transformation to a new paradigm.

Transformative experiences trigger new ways of perceiving and defining one's world. Often these experiences are life changes, for example, becoming a parent. Such a transformational experience leads individuals to redefine their roles and their purpose. The birth of a child often leads new parents to reevaluate their priorities, to become intentional about their choices, to examine their fundamental beliefs. Simply put, "When people critically examine their habitual expectations, revise them, and act on the revised point of view, transformative learning occurs. Transformative learning leads to perspectives that are more inclusive, discriminating and integrative of experience" (Cranton, 2006, p. 19). The process that we outline in the first part of this book is based upon transformative change, specifically examining our habitual practices in light of the instructional paradigm and critically examining them through the lens of the learner-centered paradigm in order to gain a new perspective.

Content and Structure of Part I

In Chapter 1 we will attempt to make a case for change by presenting the current forces affecting higher education that make the time conducive to change. In Chapter 2 we examine our current paradigm, the instructional paradigm, which is the reason we need to change. Chapter 3 provides the vision for the future, an examination of a new paradigm that can guide the shift and serve as the goal state. And finally, in Chapter 4 we present the leadership qualities that are needed to make that happen.

1

Rethinking Our Current Challenges

The Context for Change

In this chapter we will discuss the challenges in higher education that are currently creating a climate conducive to change. We will look at our opportunities for innovation through the lens that Peter Drucker (2002) offered in relation to conditions that make change possible. Drucker outlined seven areas of potential opportunity which can support innovation. Five of those are apparent in higher education today: new knowledge, changes in perception, demographic changes, industry and market changes, and process needs.

The Time for Innovation

Before we outline our strategy for undertaking this monumental task of shifting to a new paradigm, we need to make the case for making this shift at all. One of the many points that we debated as co-authors was whether it was absolutely necessary to recount the litany of stresses currently affecting higher education. Since everyone reads every day about the technological, societal, market, and political pressures on higher education, we questioned whether more discussion of these pressures would be informative, repetitive, or simply depressing for the reader.

After much thought, discussion, and coffee, we realized that we were thinking about this question from a habitual way of seeing the issues, in part because we too have read so often about these issues as *problems*. Instead of viewing these issues as negatives, the high winds and hard rains of the perfect storm intent upon sinking our ship, we reminded ourselves that storms are not solely forces of destruction but natural events that generate great power, that usher in a new weather system, that clear debris and refresh our environment. Our goal is to demonstrate how the forces that we read about and discuss on a daily basis are, in fact, power to be harnessed, opportunities for change. In Clark Kerr's 1994 analysis of the history of higher education, a history that he says gets more glorious upon reflection while fear of the future gets more dreadful, he poses the question, Why are we always so happy looking backward and so unhappy looking forward? We will undertake the challenge of looking forward, if not with complete happiness, at least with cautious optimism.

If we analyze the evolution of higher education in the United States we will see strategic junctions and times of significant challenges. In each era, academic institutions responded and took action, and higher education, subsequently, was strengthened. The calls today to reevaluate higher education are consistent with that pattern. We are at a strategic junction in which many internal and external variables are leading to questions and concerns about the relevancy of higher education, its current status, and its path to the future.

As a result, many universities, organizations, accreditation bodies, governments, and researchers are engaged in efforts to innovate. Their goal is to find ways to assure that, despite the significant challenges higher education faces, it will continue to be relevant, a key contributor to advancing knowledge and educating people for productive and successful lives. This role of higher education is necessary for sustaining a prosperous civic society. The study of the current challenges will be benefited greatly by examining colleges and universities as open systems, dynamic organisms, shaped by and shaping the environment. It is the unique structure, mission, role, and value of each university, understood in the context of the changing environment, which will allow us to address the challenges, maximize the opportunities, and also develop an enhanced vision for higher education. While there are general features and challenges common to all institutions, each institution also has unique features and challenges; there is no one-size-fits-all challenge or solution. With that in mind, we will discuss general and significant threats all institutions face, large or small, public or private. It is a time of great opportunities for those who have an interest in shaping the future of higher education, for those who, like Ernest Shackleton, maintain optimism in the face of extreme challenge.

Research on innovation and entrepreneurship demonstrates that in times of crisis or economic hardship, the opportunities for innovation increase, for the sense of crisis creates motivation for change. For example, the skyrocketing cost of gasoline in 2008 created a sense of crisis for individuals and businesses, thus creating a climate conducive to innovation in the area of alternative fuels. The sense of crisis creates a willingness and an interest in these innovations on the part of consumers and innovators, who if gas were one dollar per gallon would most likely be disinterested.

Innovative change is greater than incremental change because it results in a new condition that is measurably different from the status quo. Innovation may be achieved through the introduction of new or different policies, regulations, or practices and procedures. Our definition of innovation includes changes and processes that expand and reconceive the scope of higher education.

Management expert Peter Drucker (2002) suggests that most innovations "result from a conscious, purposeful search for innovation opportunities, which are found only in a few situations" (p. 96). He identifies seven sources of potential opportunity through which systematic analysis and knowledge can support innovation. Some are internal to organizations, for example, process needs and market changes. Others are external sources of opportunity, for example, demographic changes, new knowledge, and changes in perception. We will look at five of these innovation opportunities which offer the greatest potential for stimulating change in higher education. These forces are converging to create a climate conducive to innovation and subsequently to transformation. Drucker explains that at the heart of successful entrepreneurship is innovation: "the effort to create purposeful focused change in an enterprise's economic or social potential" (p. 96). This is achieved through "a commitment to the systematic practice of innovation"(p. 95). The future of higher education depends upon innovative entrepreneurs to lead this purposeful and focused change.

New Knowledge

The first area of potential opportunity identified by Drucker (2002) is new knowledge. New knowledge is influencing higher education on three fronts. First, discoveries and innovations are accelerating at a tremendous rate, changing discipline content and the prerequisites to adequately prepare graduates for the workplace. Especially in the sciences and technology, new knowledge is growing at an exponential rate that nearly precludes adequate preparation of graduates in our current system.

On the second front, new knowledge about how people learn is affecting our ways of teaching and preparing graduates. Many practices that have long been part of good teaching as a result of common sense and an intuitive understanding of human behavior are now part of an emerging body of research into brain functioning and learning, motivation and learning, and the role of memory as well as other affective concerns regarding power and control.

In addition, new knowledge in the form of technology is changing how we teach. Computer technology, specifically, is revolutionizing course management and delivery, and the Internet has tremendously increased the accessibility of information and changed the process of conducting research. All these forms of new knowledge are leading educators to question common pedagogical practices about what to teach as well as how to teach it. New knowledge in terms of what we teach and how we teach has provided the motivation for innovation and change.

Changes in Perception

The second area of potential opportunity identified by Drucker is changes in perception. The public perception of higher education is changing, thus creating a climate conducive to change. Once heralded as the finest educational system in the world, higher education in the United States is now perceived to be falling behind other countries and not producing qualified graduates. John Doerr, considered one of the top technology venture capitalists in the world, called education "the largest and most screwed-up part of the American economy" (quoted in Carlson & Wilmot, 2006, p. 267). Similarly, Peter Drucker said, "Thirty years from now [1997] the big university campuses will be relics. Universities won't survive.... Do you realize that the cost of higher education has risen as fast as the cost of health care? Such totally uncontrollable expenditures, without any visible improvement in either the content or the quality of education, means that the system is rapidly becoming untenable. Higher education is in deep crisis" (quoted in Carlson & Wilmot, 2006, p. 267). These and other leaders in business and industry have chimed in on the emerging public outcry for accountability in higher education. Education professors Terenzini and Pascarella (1994) called into question some of the basic tenets of American higher education. They found that educational quality did not correlate with an institution's reputation or standing. Similarly, they questioned the assumption that good researchers are good teachers, calling into question education techniques, in particular the lecture method.

In an open letter entitled *An American Imperative: Higher Expectations for Higher Education*, the Wingspread Group (1993) charged that "some faculties and institutions certify for graduation too many students who cannot read and write very well, too many whose intellectual depth and breadth are unimpressive, and too many whose skills are inadequate in the face of the demands of contemporary life" (p. 1). They conclude that "A disturbing and dangerous mismatch exists between what American society needs of higher education and what it is receiving. Nowhere is the mismatch more dangerous than in the quality of undergraduate preparation provided by many campuses" (p. 1).

In support of this claim, a National Adult Literacy Survey conducted in 1993 found that large numbers of graduates were unable to use basic skills including reading, writing, computation, and elementary problem solving (Lucas, 1994, xiii). A decade later Brown University conducted the Futures Project, a four-year examination of the major forces affecting the future of higher education. The Futures Project investigated the impact of competition and market values on higher education, targeting three specific areas: autonomy and accountability, responsibility for student learning, and access and attainment. In the report on the project, *The Future of Higher Education* (Newman, Couturier, & Scurry, 2004), the authors called for institutional responsibility with regard to student learning, claiming that at most institutions "there is an unspoken, comfortable conspiracy between faculty and students not to bother each other too much; mediocrity reigns" (p. 136).

A similar claim was made in *Declining by Degrees: Higher Education at Risk* (Hersh & Merrow, 2005), a collection of essays accompanying a PBS documentary, which exposed a lack of accountability for student learning and an unhealthy focus on research and athletics as well as other prestige factors that had little to do with educating students. Even more candid was Lewis's (2006) indictment of undergraduate education, in which he claimed that universities have forgotten their purpose, namely, creating educated adults who will take responsibility for society. In the same vein, Bok's (2005) critique of higher education's shortcomings focused both on the failure of universities to prepare citizens and the need to improve teacher quality because not enough attention is paid to pedagogy.

This is not the first time, of course, that higher education has been deemed as disaster. Lucas (1994) identified three common themes among commentators from 1965 through the 1990s: (1) professionalization of scholarship in higher education was a factor contributing to fragmentation; (2) the tendency to view knowledge as a commodity contributed to the confusion of what constituted a relevant liberal education; and (3) the structure of the university itself was a root cause of the decline. "Such allegations had been heard before, of course," said Lucas. "But they were given new clarity and force in analyses of the apparent decline of liberal educational values" (p. 268). The many critiques of the state of higher education have clarified the issues creating external pressure for changes in higher education.

Demographic Changes

The third area of potential opportunity identified by Drucker is demographic changes. Significant social, economic, and technological changes are challenging universities to reconsider their business. The profile of the undergraduate has changed dramatically. Prior to World War II, universities educated a fairly homogeneous population: 60 percent male, 97 percent Caucasian, middle and upper class backgrounds, upper third or upper quarter ranking in high school (Lucas, 1994, p. xiv). The shift in this demographic began with the GI Bill of 1944. Lucas writes, "The Serviceman's Readjustment Act of 1944—popularly dubbed the GI Bill of Rights—more than any other single initiative, brought massive changes to higher education in the postwar era" (p. xv). This influx of nontraditional students, approximately 60,000 men and women, "altered the meaning of a college education" (p. xiv).

These demographic changes continued throughout the succeeding decades. Beginning in the 1960s, women and minorities began attending college in greater numbers, and by the 1970s women out-numbered men (Lucas, 1994, p. xvi). Huber and Hutchings (2005) reported that the profile of the eighteen-year-old entering college supported by parents and working only part time has become the exception rather than the norm. Close to half of the undergradu-ates in the United States are more than twenty-four years old, and more than one quarter are working adults over thirty. The part-time student is quickly becoming the norm. Additionally, undergradu-ates who are married and/or have children have become routine. Nearly 60 percent are pursuing occupational degrees or professional studies (Lucas, 1994, p. xvi).

The nature of the traditional-aged student has also changed. Often called the *millennials*, these highly social students, techno-logically savvy and intolerant of delays, create new demands on the system from housing to admission to marketing to pedagogy. Their highly social nature leads them to prefer teamwork and group activ-ity and to keep constant contact with their social network. And with the growing calls for accessibility, more and more students are the first of their family to attend college. No longer is a homogeneous student population the norm or the goal. This changing population of students adds another new demand on institutions while offering an opportunity to support innovation.

In addition to the changing demographics of students is a shift in demographics of faculty and staff. Between 1976 and 2005 full-time nonfaculty professional staff grew at a rate of 281 percent. At the same time the rate of administrative staff doubled (American Asso-ciation of University Professors, 2008). The growth rate of full- and part-time nontenure-track faculty was 200 percent. The American Association of University Professors (2008) reports that "the more than 200 percent increase in the number of contingent faculty on the payrolls represents a deprofessionalization of the faculty role in higher education" (p. 14). Similarly, Schuster and Finkelstein (2006) write about the restructuring of the American faculty, noting that no one is content with the way campuses are governed, and the tension between managerial culture and faculty-shared governance is becoming greater, contributing to a reshaping and redistribution of academic work.

Gappa, Austin, and Trice (2007) examined what they describe as the changing context for faculty work and noted that the rise of temporary, short-term, and part-time faculty constitutes one of the "most significant responses by universities and colleges to the challenges posed by fiscal constraints and by the need to stay competitive in a rapidly changing environment" (p. 15). They conclude that the institutional goal of gaining flexibility and cost efficiency through the shifts in faculty appointment types has created an inequitable two-tiered system that undermines the sense of commitment that faculty bring to their work. These nontenure-track faculty members have little or no role in shared governance and more often than not are dividing their energy teaching at multiple institutions. In sum, the dramatic increase in administrative staff and nontenured faculty represents a major shift in university personnel that directly affects the core service of the university, academics.

Industry and Market Changes

The fourth area of potential opportunity identified by Drucker is industry and market changes. If it were not enough for institutions to respond to the changing audience, the subjects that are taught are also rapidly changing. The lines between disciplines are becoming increasingly blurred, and the rate of increase of knowledge, especially in the areas of science and technology, is in a perpetual state of acceleration. Added to that are global influences in all areas.

Business and industry have been vocal about the quality of graduates entering the workforce. A 2006 publication titled *Educating Engineers for the 21st Century: The Industry View* called for engineers to have a sound knowledge of the engineering fundamentals within their discipline as well as social and interpersonal skill sets including communication, team-working, and business skills (Spinks, Silburn, & Birchill, p. 3). Charles Vest (2007), president emeritus of MIT, called for engineering graduates to "write and communicate well, think about ethics and social responsibility, conceive and operate systems of great complexity within a framework of sustainable development and be prepared to live and work as global citizens" (p. 1).

The National Leadership Council for Liberal Education and America's Promise (LEAP; Crutcher, O'Brien, Corigan, & Schneider, 2007), an initiative sponsored by the American Association of State Colleges and Universities, identified analogous aims and outcomes for all students, regardless of discipline, outcomes necessary for survival in a twenty-first-century workforce. In preparing graduates for the twenty-first-century workforce, we need to take into consideration the features of that workforce. Kalantizis and Cope (2002) make the observation that "a division of labour into its minutest deskilled components is replaced by 'multi-skilled' all-round workers who are flexible enough to be able to do complex and integrated work" (p.20). New workers will be what they call "portfolio workers," whose strength is not in career stability and content knowledge but in range and versatility. The learning culture that will foster a transformation to the needs of the twenty-first-century workforce is one in which learning is a matter of repertoire, flexibility, and multiple talents.

Process Needs

The fifth area of potential opportunity identified by Drucker is process needs. In light of the growing concerns that our graduates are emerging from our institutions without appropriate knowledge, skills, and abilities, we must begin to question our traditional process of educating students. Our current model of undergraduate education has been based on an epistemology, methodology, and instructional paradigm focused on the transference of information and assimilation of knowledge. As technology transformation has accelerated and problems have become more complex, we have responded by adding courses that attempt to accelerate information transfer. However, it is becoming apparent that covering more or different content is not the solution.

We must begin to question the belief that knowledge in and of itself is valuable. In answering this question, more and more institutions are shifting their focus from knowledge to learning, from information transfer to helping students develop lifelong learning capacity in order to make the educational experience a transformative one. Adding more courses, transferring more information, does not transform students. Students will be transformed by increasing the depth of their learning and their self-awareness of how they learn. Our process of educating students must address this fundamental need if we are to develop lifelong learners with the capacity to readily adapt to a changing world.

While we are closer to reaching consensus on what the new graduate must know in order to succeed in the changing world and the twenty-first-century workforce, we have yet to agree on *how* those outcomes are best achieved. As Guskin and Marcy (2002) write, "Higher education now faces a critical choice about this process [by which knowledge is delivered]. Present forces in higher education will either lead to significant reform in the undergraduate educational environment or to a significant diminution in the quality of faculty work life because of sharp increases in faculty teaching loads and related work" (p. 8). Answering this question of process is an opportunity for innovation.

A Perfect Storm

These variables affecting higher education are not new. Fifty years ago, Clark Kerr, then president of the University of California system, coined the term *multiversity* to describe the transformation of the university to become increasingly responsive to market demands. In referring to the challenges facing academic leaders as a result of the explosion of knowledge and rising market demands of business, government, the military, and other groups, Lucas (1994) writes, "Too harassed to lead, university administrators had become mediators among competing interests, trying to balance contradictory demands, treating students like consumers, knowledge as a factory product and course offerings as supermarket wares" (p. 269). The intensity of these challenges has not abated in the past fifty years, but intensified.

Each of the converging challenges seems like overwhelming in its own right, but like a perfect storm, the confluence of these five challenges generates a condition or circumstance that is far more powerful. Together these five challenges have created a perfect storm, a perfect opportunity to innovate on various fronts; they have created a sense of crisis that makes innovation more likely to be accepted by those who might otherwise resist change. Academic leaders can seize the opportunity to meet these challenges and, rather than react to them, take a proactive position and use the challenges to transform higher education.

The challenges facing higher education are serious, and they will test academic leaders to be innovative and creative in moving their institutions away from the status quo. This will be achieved not through incremental change but through systemic change. Many institutions are currently implementing isolated innovations to address some of the changes discussed in this chapter. These actions, although successful on a small scale, are not addressing systemic issues. The Higher Learning Commission (HLC), the largest of the regional accrediting agencies, both in number and type of institution, provides a good gauge of the efficacy of these individual efforts. Steven D. Crow, the departing president of the HLC, noted at the 2008 annual meeting that while institutions have been working diligently to figure out what their students should be learning and whether they are, in fact, learning, it is not clear whether all the individual efforts are adding up to much (Lederman, 2008,

p. 1). Institutions are employing a wide variety of approaches, many of which are very small in scope, as they address individual challenges. Instead, leaders need to see the confluence of the challenges. Academic leaders need to assess the current situation from a comprehensive view and assume the risks required to chart a course through this perfect storm.

Transforming higher education will require innovation and a spirit of entrepreneurship. As the political, social, economic, and technological environment continues to change rapidly, more attention must be given to the role of innovation and entrepreneurship in addressing those changes. Leaders who accept this challenge will be the learning entrepreneurs, the leaders who will lead dynamic change. Drawing on an agenda put forth by Mintrom (1997) in defining policy entrepreneurs, we define learning entrepreneurs as those individuals who identify problems, shape policy, and move their institutions away from the status quo.

Recognizing that there is no single remedy or solution to the complex challenges facing institutions of higher education and that each institution has unique characteristics and features, the framework that we provide is just that, a framework, a scaffolding that will support independent investigation, an agenda to guide leaders as they take actions to innovate and redefine higher education. The comprehensive framework that we propose is predicated on the belief that in order to transform higher education, we must analyze the paradigm that we operate within. We will then call for a shift to a new paradigm, the shift toward learning-centeredness that was introduced by Barr and Tagg in 1995.

Concluding Thoughts

In describing this time of transformation, Dee Hock, former CEO of Visa Corporation, said: "We are at the very point in time when a four-hundred-year-old is dying and another is struggling to be born, a shift in culture, science, society and institutions enormously greater than the world has ever experienced" (quoted in Waldrop, 1996, p. 75). His words are reminiscent of the famous lines by English poet Matthew Arnold describing the birth of the modern era: "Wandering between two worlds, one dead,/The other powerless to be born." Both use the birth and death metaphor, a metaphor that is not only appropriate but helps to explain the emotional intensity of our situation.

The birth-and-death metaphor resonates because our institutions are organic artifacts. They live and grow and evolve as a result of the human interactions that take place within them. We use human metaphors to talk about institutions when we consider elements like growth or health of the institution. For this reason we cannot discount the human element in this enterprise, for education and leadership are all about people and relationships. As we examine the commonalities between good teaching and good leading, we will see that the core competencies for both involve human relationships, understanding people, caring about people, and developing the capacity to motivate and inspire them.

One element of the human condition is the fear of death. Even when we know that death is appropriate, a necessary condition, it's hard to let go. We become comfortable and feel safe with what we know, with what is familiar to us, and giving that up is challenging because of the uncertainty involved. To use a mundane example, think of the uncertainty we feel when the IT people take away our computer and give us an upgrade or our institution changes e-mail software. How many of us have said, "Can't I keep my old one? It works just fine." The irony is that what we are resisting isn't so much the idea of change as the need to learn something new. In order for us to thrive in the new paradigm, we must embrace change but even more important, we must embrace learning. The new paradigm is all about learning, about everyone increasing knowledge, skills, and abilities. The organization as a whole and all the members of the organizational community are learners in a perpetual state of transformation.

The anticipation and excitement of birth is also a key element of the human condition. The use of the birth metaphor for ushering in this new paradigm is apt not only because of the idea of bringing forth something new that is not completely developed, something that holds promise but is still in the progress of development, but also because one of the prevailing metaphors used in describing the role of teachers and leaders in the new paradigm is the midwife, one who attends, coaches, supports. The birth metaphor is also appropriate because birth is a transformative experience for new parents, and new parents reevaluate their priorities, become more intentional about their choices, and examine their fundamental beliefs. The birth metaphor lends a sense of continuation and evolution from the old to the new. Leaders will be challenged to allay the fears of those who will cling to the old paradigm, though it must die if we are to move forward. At the same time leaders will be challenged to inspire, to foster hope, anticipation, and excitement over the prospect of the birth of the new paradigm.

Chapter Summary

The confluence of challenges that are currently facing higher education makes this a perfect time to lead comprehensive change.

The challenges that create opportunity for innovation include the following:

- **New knowledge**, both in terms of what we teach and how we teach

- **Changes in perception** that are leading those within institutions of higher education as well as those outside to question whether we are effectively functioning, especially in regard to student learning

- **Demographic changes,** including a new generation of students, a new generation of faculty, new nonacademic professionals within higher education, changing work and study patterns of students, and growing numbers of nontraditional students

- **Industry and market changes** that are leading those who employ our graduates to call for better-skilled workers, which requires changes in what gets taught

- **Process needs** that make information transfer a less appropriate goal of higher education than teaching students how to be lifelong learners

2

The Instructional Paradigm
The Reason for Change

The first stage in leading transformational change requires us to understand our current reality. We need to know where we are before we can chart a course to a new destination. In this chapter we examine current leadership challenges in relation to the instructional paradigm, a paradigm characterized by control over individuals, ownership of knowledge, and organizational fragmentation that fosters isolation and an unhealthy competition among all members of the institution. It is difficult for us to recognize the paradigm in which we live because our practices have developed over a long time. The challenge is to understand how the paradigm has directed our thinking and our ways of operating. In this chapter we show how the instructional paradigm has dictated habits of mind that are not conducive to change or to learning. In order to transform our institutions, we must learn to become attuned to our habitual ways of working in order to realign our practices with a new paradigm, a paradigm reflective of core values focused on learning rather than instructing.

Challenges of Academic Leadership

How many of us have had someone, usually a faculty colleague, say to us, "I couldn't stand doing administrative work" or "I wouldn't want your job"? Job descriptions for administrative posts include impressive-sounding requirements like "outstanding scholar/teacher with administrative experience" and "creative visionary with proven record of academic leadership," and position descriptions talk about "leading and providing vision, leadership and oversight of the maintenance and development of quality academic programs," and promise such things as working with "a visionary president, a highly productive and engaged faculty, and an exceptionally strong senior leadership team." Yet somehow the day-to-day work seems much more humble as we spend our days and too many of our evenings and weekends running from meeting to meeting and event to event, mediating disputes that run the gamut from banal to absurd, and dividing our energy among the competing demands of students, faculty, public entities, and our immediate supervisor. The reality of the day-to-day tasks is often at odds with the ideal.

Many administrators were recruited into administration from faculty positions because of a need to help out in a time of crisis, filling a position that suddenly became vacant. That was the scenario that drew the two of us into the administrative life. Neither of us ever intended to become academic administrators; in fact, when the opportunity arose, we faced it with a healthy dose of skepticism. In spite of our reluctance to leave the classroom and our scholarly endeavors, we accepted the challenge because we were team players who wanted to help our departments in a time of need, and we also believed that we could make a difference, we could make things better through administrative channels, and in our years at this type of work, we have made things better in many ways. However, we continue to ask whether the struggle to do so has to be so great. What is it about higher education administration that makes us feel like Sisyphus, always rolling a boulder uphill? Why is it that we so often feel that our gains are minimal in relation to the effort we expend?

The leadership challenges in higher education administration differ from those of administration in the business/for-profit sector. One unique challenge of academic leadership involves the dynamic of leading peers. As we noted, a great many academic administrators began their careers as faculty and continue to hold rank and tenure in their academic departments. As academic leaders we work with our peers; they are highly intelligent individuals who have been trained to be skeptical and critical, who do not accept new ideas without challenge, and who do not necessarily hold academic leadership in high regard. One does not "boss" a tenured professor. The penchant of academics to thoughtfully consider and examine in detail every proposed change and the necessity of prolonged discussion and debate about issues make rapid response to environmental pressures nearly impossible for institutions of higher education. Yet, flexibility and rapid response to environmental factors is a requisite for survival in the twenty-first century.

A further difficulty we have in higher education is defining and measuring our outcomes, our product. A computer company or a restaurant has clearly defined goals and can usually pinpoint with fine accuracy where and how to address loss in sales or glitches in production. Higher education is being called on to perform similar feats, but creating a graduate for the twenty-first-century workforce is a very different kind of operation, one that has suffered from attempts to compare it with a factory or business enterprise.

These challenges in addition to mounting pressures for higher education to change have led to growing cynicism and frustration for all of us in higher education. Many academic administrators feel increasingly dissatisfied working within a system that at times appears to preclude change, making their effort seem unrewarding.

Rewards of Administrative Work

What are the rewards of administrative work? We asked a number of our colleagues that question, and it was a surprisingly difficult one for them to answer—their initial response was usually either sarcasm or a contemptuous snort. Some who had been involved with building renovation or procurement of necessary equipment commented on the satisfaction they felt because they had created something tangible, a physical manifestation of the work accomplished, something that people could see. So much of our work is unseen and somewhat abstract that one can lose sight of its consequences. Although a revised transfer policy affects students and the institution in many significant ways, the written document does not reflect the tremendous amount of time, energy, and negotiation it took to create it, at least not in the way that a multimillion-dollar library or a newly renovated student center does (Cullen, 2007).

In pondering this question ourselves, we agreed that for us, the greatest rewards have come from the individual students, faculty, and administrative colleagues whom we were able to support or promote in some way, such as reengaging someone in the department, publicly acknowledging someone's work or success, or assisting new members in their transition to our academic community. Regardless of the role we play within our academic community, the difference that we can make in the lives of those around us, maximizing their potential for success, will always be, for us, the most rewarding part of our work. Of the many accomplishments that we could list, our most rewarding have all dealt with situations that supported community building, collaboration, and collegiality. These examples stand out to us because the creation of community and collegiality seems to be such a difficult task to accomplish in our current system.

Lucas (1994) notes a recurring theme regarding loss of community in late twentieth-century commentaries on higher education. He points to George Douglas's analysis as the most insightful of many during this period. Douglas commented that universities were failing to provide the type of human setting in which education worthy of the term could thrive. They were too big, too full of activity to be places of authentic learning. Instead he claimed they had become *factories* for producing specialized expertise or for imparting information. The prevailing opinion in the 1990s was that the sheer size of modern universities militated against the creation of community (Lucas, 1994, p. 288).

We would argue that the frustration of working in higher education, in a system that seems to preclude change, is not solely the result of the size of institutions, but rather that it is caused by the paradigm that governs all institutions, large and small. The instructional paradigm we work in is not conducive to community nor to individuality or creativity. In fact, it is at odds with most of the values espoused by today's colleges and universities. It is a paradigm that has fostered alienation and an unhealthy divisiveness between and among faculty and administration as well as between academics and nonacademics within institutions. Our paradigm must change if higher education is to change.

The Instructional Paradigm

The values, attitudes, and biases inherent in the instructional paradigm are predicated upon an industrial model of human learning. This factory model of education values quality control, which is ironic since higher education is currently under such intense scrutiny to be accountable for the quality of graduates. Concern over the business/factory influence on higher education is certainly not new. John Jay Chapman wrote in 1909, "The men who stand for education and scholarship have ideals of business men. . . . They are, in truth, business men. The men who control [universities] today are very little else than businessmen running a large department store which dispenses education to the millions" (quoted in Lucas, 1994, p. 192). Most of the critics of the growing bureaucracy in higher education admitted that it could not be eliminated, but still decried its current form which had a tendency to "dehumanize collegiate life" (Lucas, 1994 p. 193). A more recent criticism in a report issued by the American Association of University Professors (2008) placed the factory analogy in contemporary perspective as U.S. colleges and universities "are embracing the operating strategies of for-profit corporations with growing fervor. . . . [C]olleges and universities increasingly conceptualize higher education as a commodity and attempt to provide it at the lowest cost. They do so by reorganizing themselves as 'knowledge factories' in which a variety of internal functions (for example, dining services and facilities maintenance) are outsourced to for-profit contractors who pay their workers minimum wages and in which the central teaching and research functions are outsourced to legions of poorly paid nontenure-track adjunct faculty, postdoctoral fellows, and graduate students" (p. 12). Similarly, Dolence and Norris (1995) described the transition from the industrial age to the information age, noting that the factory model that characterized education in the industrial age was insufficiently flexible and focused on outputs and processes rather than on learning (p. 6).

In this factory model, students' potential is determined by ACT, SAT, HSGPA, and sometimes other quantifiable measures. Depending upon our institutional standards, students are deemed to be the acceptable quality of raw material for our product. Quality control is especially evident in the freshman year, during which the weaker material is sorted out. The Wingspread Group on Higher Education (1993) charged that "Our education system is better organized to discourage students—to weed them out—than it is to cultivate and support our most important national resource, our people" (p. 5). Students are directed to take a prescribed collection of courses in a prescribed sequence in order to assure quality control over the exiting product, our graduates. This model devalues the individual. In the mass production mentality that this model represents, students assimilate information at equivalent rates with equivalent responses, thus creating like products. This assembly line of education presupposes a sameness to individuals, so that regardless of prior learning, individual differences, or extracurricular experiences, each student following a like path will emerge from the assembly line like all the others.

A Paradigm of Control

The instructional paradigm is a paradigm of control. It is not supportive of leadership and innovation. In it, everyone is controlled by someone. Students are controlled by professors who hold the power of the grade. Learning is an assimilative process whereby the professor, the owner of knowledge, dispenses it to the students. The professor holds power and control over the students, who must meet the expectations of the professor whether or not those expectations were clearly delineated or articulated. Students are discouraged from collaborating in this competitive environment. They are judged on their individual abilities in competition with the others in the class. The teacher is not a facilitator or mentor but, rather, a judge and, often, a gatekeeper.

Junior faculty find themselves in a similar situation as they begin becoming acculturated into the system. The *Harvard Study of New Scholars* (Trower & Bleak, 2002), a study of the dissatisfaction that junior faculty experience, reported that junior faculty are increasingly discontented in this authoritarian environment in which there is one way of knowing, one way of conducting research, one way to assimilate into a department or unit, one way to demonstrate success, and one way to achieve tenure and rank.

It's interesting to think about what it means to administer in the traditional paradigm. The synonyms of the word *administer* in the thesaurus provide an interesting view of our perceived function: *manage, direct, run, order, control, oversee,* and our favorite, *do paperwork.* This list of synonyms illustrates the definition of the perceived role of the administrator in our current paradigm.

Ownership of Knowledge

This instructional paradigm views knowledge as a quantifiable commodity that can be isolated, identified, and controlled. In the traditional division of units, departments, and colleges according to academic discipline, the knowledge is owned by the discipline. Tagg (2003) writes that faculty as the core of educational institutions have been replaced by departments and that their influence on student learning is exercised through academic departments: "At most colleges, academic departments hire faculty members, and academic departments in the Instructional Paradigm college derive their power from their role as depositories for classes. Administrations, to the extent they are involved in undergraduate education, are largely structures for organizing and channelling the activities of departments" (p. 23).

This ownership of knowledge dictates various processes within the university, among them hiring, promotion and merit, and curriculum development. The very concept of shared governance has at its roots ownership of discipline knowledge.

The core belief of shared governance is that faculty, because of their academic expertise and their long-term commitment to individual institutions (as opposed to academic administrators and governing board members whose terms at institutions are often relatively short in comparison to that of faculty), should govern the academic functions of their institutions, including the regulation of academic standards and curriculum and the hiring of faculty and staff. The purpose of shared governance is to maintain academic integrity by preventing political or commercial interests from influencing institutional decision making. One of the safeguards against outside pressure is the individual academic's responsibility to maintain standards set by his or her discipline-specific professional organizations. The adherence to academic standards established by discipline, rather than by individual institution, was intended to provide balance and integrity of standards across institutions. While we would never argue against the importance of shared governance, shared governance within the instructional paradigm has contributed to a mindset that has fostered unnecessary divisiveness and fragmentation. As Vartan Gregorian writes, "Schools should not be treating each other as isolated silos, because the strength of the university is in its totality" (quoted in Hersh & Merrow, 2005, p. 94).

We can see the effect of this belief that knowledge is both owned and distributable in the curriculum review process; in some instances, professors are asked to delineate how many minutes per semester will be devoted to individual topics within the course outline, or accrediting bodies ask for the number of hours per semester devoted to specific knowledge. Tagg (2003) referred to this as educational atomism: "In the 'educational atomism' of the Instruction Paradigm, the parts of the teaching and learning process are seen as discrete entities. The parts exist prior to and independent of any whole; the whole is no more than the sum of the parts, or even less. The college interacts with students only in discrete, isolated environments, cut off from one another because the parts—the classes—are prior to the whole. A 'college education' is the sum of the student's experience of a series of discrete, largely unrelated, three-credit classes" (p.110).

This view of knowledge and education cannot keep pace with the incredible rate of change in the twenty-first-century workforce. Many fields now cannot accelerate the transfer of information to students fast enough to keep up with the rate of change in the knowledge of the discipline. It is estimated, for example, that by the time engineering graduates walk across the stage with their diplomas, nearly half of the knowledge of their discipline is obsolete. When the focus is on knowledge rather than on learning, obsolescence is inevitable.

A Paradigm of Isolation

The industrial model of the instructional paradigm is driven by competition, and this emphasis on competition fosters isolation. Students compete against one another within classes for grades. The competition among students for seats in certain high-profile programs exacerbates an overemphasis on grades and test scores at the expense of learning, encouraging students to take safe and easy choices in order to achieve the highest GPA. The same competition is fostered among faculty, who are judged in isolation for tenure, promotion, and merit by systems that, more often than not, privilege solo scholarship over collaborative works. And if faculty do collaborate, the hierarchy of lead author undercuts the concept of true collaboration. There may be no one more isolated than academic administrators, who find themselves isolated from the faculty they supervise and often isolated from one another because of the need to compete for resources and influence within the system.

Perhaps the greatest sense of isolation is derived from the unfortunate dichotomy between administration and faculty that pervades the instructional paradigm. Too often faculty and administration appear to be working at odds with one another and seeing higher education from competing vantage points. The current paradigm leads to a lack of trust, which is nowhere more apparent than in the pervasive distrust between faculty and administration that is fostered by the instructional paradigm.

In the instructional paradigm, when a faculty member makes the transition to an administrative position, he or she, as well as others, often perceive the transition as moving to a different world and worldview. Faculty members often joke with their peers who move into administrative posts, saying things like "You've gone to the dark side," in spite of the reality that most academic administrators retain their faculty status or hold tenure in an academic department. Stephen Brookfield (2006) examines what he labels "cultural suicide" in relation to adult learners who find themselves questioning their learning process because their family, peers, and social group act as if they have betrayed them by their choice to be a student, by making the choice to change. Although Brookfield's discussion is related to students from minority groups or working class backgrounds, there is a strong parallel here to the faculty member who moves into administration. The person who makes this choice is sometimes seen as betraying the values and culture of his or her professional community. Brookfield describes students in this situation as feeling that their identities have been challenged, that they have become alienated from their families and social group.

The perceived divide between faculty and administration is at the very core of the problems we witness with the instructional paradigm. In the instructional paradigm, the faculty member who leaves the faculty position to become an administrator abandons the role of faculty and presumably adopts a new a set of values and ideals that are perceived to be in conflict with those previously held as a faculty member.

The overemphasis on competition and control in the instructional paradigm betrays a lack of respect for, as well as a fundamental distrust of, the individual. A colleague once described his institution as a place that valued jobs but not the people in them. Individuals at this institution typically became more embittered as the years passed because of the processes and decision making that perpetuated a climate of disrespect for all employees, faculty and staff alike. In places like this, rules and policies predominate; fear of legal reprisal governs decision making. At this institution legal counsel was so powerful that the university counsel sat next to the president on the stage at commencement. The prevailing attitude in the instructional paradigm is that students, faculty, and staff need to be controlled by rules, processes, and practices, which is demoralizing and limits creativity and innovation.

Working Habits in the Instructional Paradigm

Senge's (1990) characterization of controlling organizations mirrors the values of the instructional paradigm. In his preface to the revised edition of *The Fifth Discipline*, Senge quotes Edward Deming: "Our prevailing system of management has destroyed our people. People are born with intrinsic motivation, self-respect, dignity, curiosity to learn and joy in learning. The forces of destruction begin with toddlers—a prize for the best Halloween costume, grades in school, gold stars—and go on up through the university. . . . We will never transform the prevailing system of management without transforming our prevailing system of education. They are the same system" (xii–xiii).

Among the elements of traditional or controlling organizations that Senge (1990) identified were managing by fear, which results in focusing first on pleasing the boss (or teacher); dualistic thinking regarding right versus wrong answers, which results in overemphasis on technical problem solving; predictability and controllability evidenced in the belief that managing is controlling; and a recognition that excessive competitiveness leads to distrust—all of which leads to organizational fragmentation. Senge (1990) sees that leadership in traditional, controlling organizations is predicated upon a belief in people's powerlessness, their need to be directed and led. This characterization of the traditional, controlling organization all too accurately describes the workplace governed by the instructional paradigm, the system that Deming claimed has destroyed our people.

Administrators Rendered Powerless

As administrators within this system, we too find ourselves rendered powerless either by those above us in the organizational structure or by our own policies and procedures. How many times has a department head delivered unpopular information to his or her department with the only explanation being "I have no power to change this" or "This is out of my control"? How many times has a dean been presented with an innovative idea by a faculty member only to respond, "That's a great idea but our system can't accommodate it"? How many times do academic administrators find themselves modifying or accepting less than optimal conditions for learning because of policies or decisions made by other divisions within the institution, whether it's the custodial crew determining classroom arrangements or the computer software system driving curriculum configurations? From our experiences at varying levels of administration in multiple institutions, we would answer, "too often." In part, this sense of powerlessness has arisen from a rise in professionalization of nonacademic functions within the university. The American Association of University Professors (2008) describes this movement:

For most of the history of U.S. higher education, faculty members performed the key administrative functions. The college president, dean of faculty, dean of students, and director of admissions were professors who simultaneously wore faculty and administrative hats. The bird's-eye view of the institution's different functions that faculty administrators had gave them an advantage in understanding the pedagogical consequences of administrative decisions, and their institutions benefited from the broad base of knowledge. In the post–World War II years, however, college and university enrollments grew dramatically, and specialization increasingly characterized professional administrative staff positions. This movement away from generalists and toward specialists has accelerated during the past twenty years, creating a disconnect between administrations and academic progress. As a result administrators sometimes do not appreciate the effects their decisions will have across other parts of the institution. (p. 12–13)

Lack of Logic Becomes the Norm

The instructional paradigm is a habit. We have become accustomed to the routine regardless of how illogical it might be. Hackman (2002), in writing about how teams work, states that "mindless reliance on habitual routines results in suboptimal performance" (p. 173). For example, because our budget is determined by the previous year's spending level, we spend down our budgets even in times of fiscal hardship, because if we spend less, our budget allotment will decrease. The illogic of the system promotes illogic among those who must work within the system for survival. Because of the extreme amount of work it takes to change even minor policies or procedures, we too often capitulate because of competing demands upon our time and resources. We resort to fixing things within our sphere of influence. Solving problems in the instructional paradigm is like repairing a part on a machine. Everyone understands what the solution or answer is and simply awaits implementation so that the system will be back online and functioning once the solution is implemented. In this model the administrator is a repair person, a fixer of problems. When we are not playing the role of repair person, we are playing the role of fire control technician, putting out fires.

When individuals feel a loss of control, they lose their internal motivation, which subsequently undermines job performance. Zull (2002) examined control in relation to brain function, noting that the brain seeks to constantly be in control, and this causes humans to make decisions that give them control regardless of whether they fully comprehend the implications of their decisions. The instructional paradigm does not foster creative problem solving or innovative thinking. In this paradigm we defer to policy and to precedent. The oppressiveness of this paradigm leads to "working the system" regardless of the logic or to micromanaging since the larger issues are out of our control.

Novels about academia make fun of academic institutions through absurdity that often hits way too close to home. The main character in Richard Russo's *Straightman* (1997) explains to his creative writing class that comedy and tragedy don't go together, but then he concedes that that has not been his experience in academe. In the novel, the inability of the campus president to release a budget for the coming year compounded by the impending layoffs at the institution lead the main character, the interim head of the English department, to hold a campus duck hostage in front of TV cameras in order to gain the public acknowledgement of the problem he faces without a budget since within the system no one is willing or able to make such an acknowledgement.

Although taking a duck hostage while wearing fake nose and glasses is clearly over the top, the situation which leads to the comedic scene is all too familiar. Institutional inability to react to outside pressures too often leads administrators at the top of the hierarchy to become paralyzed and those at the bottom of the hierarchy to act out of desperation.

Unmaking the Paradigm

Since Barr and Tagg (1995) introduced the idea of a paradigm shift from an instructional paradigm that emphasizes teaching as delivery of knowledge to a learner-centered paradigm that emphasizes student learning and construction of knowledge, faculties nationwide have made significant strides in reorienting their teaching strategies toward the learner-centered model. The institutional shift that Barr and Tagg called for was not confined to classroom practices; yet, very little discussion has taken place regarding the magnitude of systemic change beyond the classroom about what a true paradigm shift would involve.

Perhaps one reason why the shift toward learner-centeredness has had greater success in the classroom is that teaching, in either paradigm, is empowering and adaptable. To a great degree professors have autonomy in their classrooms, which allows them from multiple paths to reach desired outcomes; they have control over their courses, which allows them to be flexible, creative, and responsive to change. If one method of teaching isn't getting the desired outcome, the professor can simply try another strategy. Academe outside of the individual classroom is far less flexible, and this inflexibility is one of the greatest challenges facing higher education today as institutions attempt to respond to the numerous calls for accountability.

As academic administrators we enjoy talking about the impressive strides that our institutions are making in bringing about this shift; we publicize innovative successes, and we write mission statements and planning documents that reflect our new emphasis on accountability for learning and our commitment to student learning, yet we rarely discuss how *our* practices as academic leaders must change for this shift to be complete. It is important for academic administrators to consider how the paradigm shift will change our roles because the shift in emphasis from teaching to learning will change administrative responsibilities and the way we perceive our roles. The magnitude of organizational change will require self-assessment and self-conscious attention to all practices within the institution. In fact, we will argue that the institutional shift toward learner-centeredness cannot be achieved without academic leaders who fully understand the concept of the learner-centered paradigm and who are willing to reconsider their roles in light of this new paradigm and to adopt administrative practices that reflect the culture and values of the learner-centered paradigm, taking actions which help to push forward the learner-centered agenda in order for the shift to be truly institutional and complete.

In *The Learning Paradigm College* (2003), Tagg examines the barriers to transforming higher education; in doing so, he writes of the *tenacity* of paradigms. Paradigms are tenacious because they are invisible, part of the structure that guides our reasoning and our actions. They are the air we breathe, our scaffolding, our sense of stability. He likens them to a lens, a language, or a habit. But Tagg reminds us that paradigms can be changed: "It is an artifact of human ingenuity. We made it and sustain it. We can unmake it" (2003, p. 308). Unmaking the paradigm is, in part, what this book is about. In unmaking the paradigm, we must first examine the lens that we see through, for it is a corrective lens. It makes accommodations for our natural sight in order that we achieve 20/20 vision, so that we see like everybody else. In unmaking the paradigm, we will need to take off our corrective lenses so that we can learn to see anew.

The instructional paradigm is our first language. We don't remember how we learned it; we may not understand the grammatical structures that underpin it, but we know it and use it with great facility. Whether we believe that our language shapes our thought or our thought shapes our language, the rules of our language, our syntax and vocabulary, betray the attitudes and beliefs of our culture. For example, when feminists challenged the use of *he* as the universal pronoun in English, the challenge was not a simple matter of vocabulary; the use of *he* to refer to both genders represented a deeply ingrained attitude in our culture regarding an imbalance of power between males and females. Challenging its use was challenging the culture, and drawing attention to it created a sense of self-consciousness among language users attuned to the issue. Talking about paradigms as languages is a very useful metaphor, for in unmaking our paradigm, many of our deeply held convictions, standards, and practices will be challenged. We will become self-conscious. We will learn a new language in the process, one in which the syntax and grammatical categories reflect our new cultural attitudes. We learn second languages differently from the way we learn first languages, by conscious attention to the grammatical structures of the new languages and learning to apply them through continued practice. So in order to learn to speak in the new paradigm, we will have to be always conscious of the new underlying structures which will guide our development and consciously practice thinking and operating according to the new rules.

And the instructional paradigm is a habit. How do we break a habit? First we have to recognize it, and then we become self-conscious about it, even obsessed by it, in order to change. Breaking a habit, whether it's a habit of speech, a comfortable routine, or a self-destructive behavior, requires intentionality, concerted thought, and self-awareness. It requires tenacity too. But once we break a habit, we feel freed from a routine that had dominated our behavior; we feel empowered by our stamina and will power that allowed us to win over our impulses, to break the habit. We feel energized and invigorated by our new beginning. But as any of us who have tried to break a habit know, habits aren't broken easily. Learning to see and understand the underlying assumptions of our paradigm is no easy task, as Brookfield (1995) writes, "Paradigmatic assumptions are the hardest of all assumptions to uncover. They are the structuring assumptions we use to order the world into fundamental categories. Usually we don't even recognize them as assumptions, even after they've been pointed out to us. Instead we insist that they're objectively valid renderings of reality, the facts as we know them to be true" (p. 2).

Unmaking the paradigm is a challenge, but it can be achieved. Through a systematic and comprehensive review of our institutional processes for the purpose of examining whether they are governed by the instructional paradigm and how they might be redesigned to become compatible with the learner-centered paradigm, leaders, grounded in learning theory and inspired by the optimism of a new beginning, can transform higher education.

Concluding Thoughts

A colleague sent us a news story while we were in the midst of writing this book, and it can serve as an analogy for the challenge that stands before us. It was a story about Japanese farmers developing a square watermelon. Japanese grocery stores as well as refrigerators are smaller than those in the United States, and conventional watermelons took up too much space. So, in response, the Japanese farmers developed a square watermelon. This newly shaped fruit looked unusual, like nothing ever seen before, but was easier to ship, easier to store, and commanded a premium price. The moral of the story has everything to do with shifting paradigms, giving us three guiding principles as we seek to effect comprehensive change:

1. Don't assume. Just because we are accustomed to round watermelons doesn't mean that another shape isn't possible. Just because we are accustomed to defining our work in higher education one way, doesn't mean another shape isn't possible.

2. Question habits. If we do not break our habits and become intentional about our work, we will never change. We will

simply continue our habitual behaviors and wonder why everything stays the same.

3. Be creative. The task of adopting a new paradigm requires individuals to see everything anew, see from different perspectives and see the possibilities.

Chapter Summary

Frustrations with academic administrative work are rooted in the instructional paradigm that governs policy and procedure.

The instructional paradigm

- fosters divisiveness among all constituents but most negatively between administration and faculty.

- functions under the assumption that control is necessary.

- devalues individuality and creativity.

- operates on a factory model of learning.

- refers competition to collaboration.

- results in organizational fragmentation.

- fosters dualistic thinking and technical problem solving.

Once we learn to see the paradigm that controls us, we can unmake it by paying close attention to our habitual ways of working and realigning our practices with a new paradigm.

3

The Learner-Centered Paradigm

The Goal of Change

The goal of Chapter 2 was to show why change is needed by providing insight to the instructional paradigm that governs our thinking. The goal of this chapter is to describe the goal of change by providing an overview of the learner-centered paradigm. Most of the progress toward learner-centeredness to date has been in the classroom, so by looking at the classroom practices in the new paradigm, we can gain a clearer understanding of how the new paradigm functions. If we are to see our institutions as learner-centered, then the learner-centered classroom can function as a microcosm of the institution as a whole. The learner-centered teacher serves as an illustration of the best practices to be adopted by teachers and administrators within the new paradigm.

In this chapter we will examine teaching practices as they apply to leadership skills. Specifically we will look at strategies learner-centered teachers employ to share power; how their consideration of students' prior learning affects current learning; how they design learning opportunities that empower students and encourage active learning; and how they use assessment to monitor their effectiveness. Before we look at teaching strategies, we will begin with a brief overview of the characteristics of the learner-centered paradigm and the research about learning upon which it is based in order to make the case for why this knowledge is necessary for academic leaders.

The Learner-Centered Paradigm

In making the distinction between the instructional and learner-centered paradigms, John Tagg (2003) noted that in the instructional paradigm time is constant but learning varies. In other words, the fifty-minute period for a class is the constant but how much students learn in that time is variable. In the learner-centered paradigm, learning becomes the constant and time becomes the variable. Rather than focusing on our delivery of information, how many minutes we devote to transmitting knowledge on a particular subject, assuming that all individuals will assimilate at a constant rate, the focus is on the individual learner and assessing when the learner has actually achieved specified learning outcomes regardless of the time it takes. Unlike the instructional paradigm, the learner-centered paradigm values people and individual differences, collaboration and team work, placing learning rather than knowledge at the center of all decisions. Individuals' varying backgrounds and previous experiences inform the learning process and enrich collaboration. If the metaphor for the instructional paradigm is the factory, the metaphor for the learner-centered paradigm is the community. In this paradigm individuals rely on one another, support one another, and learn from one another.

An understanding of the learner-centered paradigm will provide academic leaders with a vision for the future, a guide and a goal. In the grammar of the instructional paradigm, *knowledge* is the subject and *control* is the verb. In the learner-centered paradigm, *learning* is the subject and *collaborate* is the verb. Extending the second-language metaphor from Chapter 2, knowledge of the learner-centered classroom will be the grammar of our new language. As we assess our roles and how we lead in the new paradigm, we will need to refer back to our grammar to know how to speak in this new language. We will need to become self-conscious about our vocabulary, quite literally. As leaders of institutions, we will function like teachers in the learner-centered classroom, so it is essential that we understand the major differences between the instructional paradigm understanding of the teacher's role and the learner-centered one.

Research on Learning

The learner-centered paradigm, as introduced by Barr and Tagg (1995), portrays an educational environment that is holistic and empowering, focused on learning rather than knowledge. Literature on learning is extensive, and as Weimer (2002) explains in her literature review of learner-centered instructional practice, it spans decades and crosses disciplines. She writes, "Interest in learning may be recent, but the study of it is not" (p. 7).

The learner-centered paradigm is based upon emerging research that has informed our understanding of how people learn. The past two decades have been rich in research on cognition, learning, and how the brain works. Work by biologists like Leamnson (1999), Sylwester (1995), and Zull (2002) has aided in defining the brain's functions in relation to learning. Distinctions between memory, knowledge, and depth of knowing have been characterized by such researchers as Marton and Saljo (1976); Marton, Hounsell, and Entwistle (1977); Entwistle and Entwistle (1991); Ramsden (1988, 1992); Langer (1997); and Bowden and Marton (1998). And psychologists and educational researchers (Bandura [1986, 1993, 1994, 1997]; Biggs [1999]; Gardner [1983]; Csikszentmihalyi [1990]; Covington [1992]; Conway, Perfect, Anderson, Gardiner, & Cohen [1997]; Dweck & Licht [1980]; Dweck [2006]) have contributed greatly to our understanding of the role of memory, self-regulation, self-efficacy, and motivation in regard to learning. We know more than ever before about how people learn, what inhibits learning, and different kinds of learning. This knowledge is the basis upon which the new paradigm is built.

This emerging view of learning balances an interest in individual differences with the role of learning in a social context. A considerable body of literature supports the notion that the students' conceptions of their own abilities influence their ability to learn. Bandura (1986, 1993, 1994, 1997) studied the academic impact of self-efficacy and learning, demonstrating among other things that the teacher's belief in the students' efficacy affected student achievement. In summarizing the implication for learning derived from the substantial body of research on self-efficacy, Stage, Muller, Kinzie, and Simmons (1998) conclude, "When faculty (1) construe ability as an acquirable skill, (2) deemphasize competitive social comparisons and highlight self-comparison of progress and personal accomplishment, and (3) reinforce an individual student's ability to exercise some control over the learning environment, enhanced self-efficacy is likely to occur" (p. 30). This finding supports the learner-centered emphasis on establishing community, sharing power, and using assessment and evaluation to reach specific learning outcomes.

The learner-centered paradigm is built upon constructivist philosophy, which is advanced from Piaget's dynamic constructivist theory of knowing (von Glaserfeld, 1995, p. 6). However, the label *constructivism* takes various forms, such as radical constructivism (von Glaserfeld), social constructionism (Gergen), social cultural constructivism (Bruner), and social constructivism (Vygotsky). Generally speaking, constructivists believe that learners construct knowledge rather than receive it and the act of construction is greatly dependent upon the prior knowledge and experience that the learner brings to the task. Von Glaserfeld (1995) explains, "[F]rom the constructivist perspective, learning is not a stimulus-response phenomenon. It requires self-regulation and the building of conceptual structures through reflection and abstraction" (p. 14). In this construction of knowledge, active engagement, problem solving, and contextual relevance all play an integral role. Social constructivists, particularly, employ teaching strategies that foster collaboration and social learning opportunities. They stress that collaboration among learners is more productive than independent learning because of the construction of knowledge through varying backgrounds of the community members (Bruffee, 1993). Key here is the importance of relevance to learning and again establishing a sense of a community of learners.

Another educational philosophy informing the learner-centered approach is that of Paulo Freire (2003). His philosophy as expressed in *Pedagogy of the Oppressed* emphasizes student-centered learning. His educational philosophy is grounded in his concept of *conscientization*, which refers to students attaining a deepened awareness of the sociocultural reality of their lives and their ability to take action to transform that reality. Also transformed is the relationship between student and teacher. Eradicating the authoritarian model of professor lecturing to student, Freire calls for teachers and students to be co-investigators and co-learners in the learning process and as such to share power and control of the learning environment.

Stage, Muller, Kinzie, and Simmons (1998) explore the connection between Freire's philosophy and service learning, one of the active learning strategies of the learner-centered pedagogy: "Some connections between a service-learning approach to teaching and Freire are immediately evident. For example, service-learning programs provide a learning context that parallels many aspects of Freire's theory about learning. Service learning allows instructors and students to engage in dialogue, instructors and students are co-investigators in the learning process, and instructor and learner are jointly responsible for learning. The emphasis of conscientization and service-learning on critical reflection also creates a natural connection between Freire's theory and service learning" (p. 90).

Active learning pedagogies grow out of Friere's philosophy as well as social constructivism. Such pedagogical strategies include problem-based learning, service learning, and activities that promote relevance for the learner, as well as ownership and control over the process of learning. In sum, knowledge is not owned and disseminated; rather, it is constructed by learners. Teachers are designers and stewards of learning environments, and learners are in control of their own learning which they do through collaboration rather than competition. Individual differences are not only accepted but needed for the synergy of collaboration to function best.

Why We Need to Know Learner-Centered Practices

As leaders of the shift to a learner-centered paradigm, we need to understand the philosophy and practices of the learner-centered classroom for a variety of reasons. First, in terms of discovering new patterns of behavior as leaders, we will use the learner-centered teacher as a model, for teaching and leading share common traits. In reevaluating our core values and practices, we will do so by realigning them with learner-centered values, keeping in mind the goal of establishing community, sharing power, and using assessment and evaluation to reach outcomes.

On a more practical level, in our role as supervisors we must be knowledgeable regarding the practices of those we supervise. In order to give formative and useful feedback on teaching, we need to know what we are observing and what the outcomes and goals are as well as the role that assessment and evaluation play. In Chapter 7 we will provide some practical suggestions for classroom observation.

Likewise, in our role as community builders, we need to know enough about how the learner-centered pedagogy works in order to allay the fears of colleagues who do not yet understand the transition and fear that the teaching norms of their department are being threatened. We have each witnessed cases in which departments became embroiled over the pedagogical strategies employed by members new to the department. In one case, the new faculty member released her class for one week so that students could meet in groups to work on assigned projects in the library, where she would monitor and be available for support. The person's tenure review committee was outraged that her classes were not meeting and called for the person's dismissal based upon a "lack of professionalism."

The tenure review committee in this case was so entrenched in the fifty-minute modules of the instructional paradigm that they could simply not conceive of the idea that learning could take place in a setting outside of the classroom. Especially in institutions that identify themselves as teaching institutions, the norms of departmental pedagogy can become contentious.

It will be the responsibility of academic leaders to guide faculty development efforts in order to transform departmental cultures, particularly in regard to a focus on learning. Learner-centered teaching also requires different kinds of support than instructional-based delivery. As leaders, we need to understand this so that we can provide for and advocate for the support needed for this kind of teaching.

The Learner-Centered Classroom

If we accept that an institution as a whole is learning-centered, then the learning-centered class serves as a microcosm of the learning-centered university. In other words, a learning-centered institution should reflect on a large scale the qualities that we expect to find in a learning-centered class. So, let's take a look at learner-centered teaching in order to clarify the ways it is different from its instructional paradigm counterpart.

In her book *Learner-Centered Teaching*, Maryellen Weimer (2002) outlines five key changes in practice that occur when teachers move to a learner-centered pedagogy: (1) balance of power, (2) function of content, (3) role of the teacher, (4) responsibility for learning, and (5) purpose and process of evaluation. We will offer a brief introduction to these concepts and consider how these changes in teaching practice might be applied to administrative practices.

Balance of Power

A colleague was teaching her class one day. Her students were in groups, talking and engaged in lively debate about the project at hand. She circulated among the groups redirecting conversation where necessary and answering questions. Suddenly one of her colleagues appeared in the doorway and motioned to her. He asked, "Do you need help getting your class under control?" Completely taken by surprise, she smiled and thanked him replying, "No. This class is doing extremely well with this project. Thank you." Later the department head stopped by her office to ask how her classes were going. He confessed that some of her colleagues were concerned that her classes seemed "out of control."

The use of the phrase *out of control* is indicative of the instructional paradigm's notions of what a "good" class should look like. Too many times tenured colleagues or department heads who review the teaching of junior faculty instruct them to "do something I can observe," the subtext of which is "Lecture; let me see how well you perform." The learner-centered classroom is not focused on the performance of the teacher but rather the performance of the learner. Sharing power and control can promote engagement and subsequently facilitate learning.

The balance of power is related to motivating students to learn. Research in psychology has shown that intrinsic motivation to learn is affected by individuals' personal interests as well as their sense of choice and control. "Intrinsic motivation is also facilitated on tasks that are comparable to real-world situations and meet needs for choice and control. Educators can encourage and support learners' natural curiosity and motivation to learn by attending to individual differences in learners' perceptions of optimal novelty and difficulty, relevance, and personal choice and control" (American Psychological Association, 2008, para. 10).

With power and control comes responsibility. The predominant way to motivate students in the instructional paradigm is through grades. Professors hold power over students through grading; though ironically, for most faculty members, grading is the part of their job they enjoy the least. We have all witnessed students who pay more attention to the point system than they do to the course content or experienced the aggravation of trying to motivate students who are very content to just pass with a C or D. In the learner-centered paradigm, one means of stimulating motivation for learning is through sharing control.

The idea of giving up control is somewhat controversial and deserves clarification. Stephen Brookfield (1995) cautions that professors have an ethical responsibility to hold on to their power, that sharing power and providing students with opportunities to make decisions is not the same as giving up power. Cranton (2006) explains that students are so accustomed to being completely powerless that even small opportunities for decision making make a tremendous difference. She writes, "Educators can support learner empowerment in many ways, most of which exist in the small, ordinary, everyday interactions of the teaching and learning environment" (p. 133). In short, we have to teach empowerment rather than simply relinquish responsibility, and this can be done by incrementally increasing opportunities for decision making on the part of the learner. There are various ways of doing this, such as inviting students to have some say in course policies, giving students optional avenues for meeting learning outcomes, or providing means for students to give input about course content. Even something as simple as asking which of two articles they would prefer to read for an assignment offers them unaccustomed decision-making power. Faculty are experimenting with this concept with great success.

Sample Teaching Practice

Professor B is an experienced history professor whose courses are known for being writing intensive as well as technology rich. After taking part in a faculty learning community at her university, she decided to revamp her courses with a new goal of sharing power and control. She built choice and class decision making in several ways. First, when she handed out her syllabus to the students on the first day, she explained that she was not going to read the syllabus to them. Instead, they would be writing an essay analyzing the syllabus, drawing on examples from it to illustrate what their expectations were of the course and of her. She gave them a few minutes to pre-view it to see if they had any initial questions. Almost immediately a young man raised his hand and asked, "What's this mean, 'atten-dance to be negotiated by class'?" Professor B responded that the class would come to an agreement with her on what they deemed to be a fair attendance policy. She then pointed out that the same was true for the policy on late work. The students looked confused. The same young man raised his hand again and said, "That's *your* job." Unruffled by the young man's tone, she smiled and responded, "It doesn't have to be." Other students began to comment on the idea more favorably. Another fellow queried with a smug smile, "What if we say the policy is that there isn't an attendance policy?" She quickly replied, "A policy of no policy is still a policy. If you don't want me to take attendance, that's your choice as a class. I will tell you my experiences of the pros and cons of attendance policies, and you can decide for yourselves whether you think you need to have attendance be a factor in your grade." In the next class period when the negotiation of policies took place, the class decided that they did not want to have attendance count against their grades, but they conceded that daily work the students missed could not be made up. They also negotiated an interesting policy on late work that was tied to readiness for peer review sessions that were sched-uled before each paper was due. Their policy was actually stricter than Professor B's former policy on late work. Professor B also pro-vided students with choices. She gave them multiple options for achieving learning outcomes in the course and options on topics for assignments. These options were all explained in the syllabus.

The syllabus essays provided interesting insights regarding the students' responses to sharing power. Professor B couldn't get over the fact that they expressed themselves in the very language that the research used in describing the impact of power and control. They said things like "No one has ever treated us like adults before" and "This professor trusts us." Professor B found that the syllabus assignment established a tone for the class, one of trust and also one of responsibility. As the semester progressed, there were students who abused the attendance policy and fell behind, but when they talked with her in conference about their situation, not a single one blamed her or tried to negotiate a new deal. To a person, they said, "It's my own fault." Professor B's analysis of the changes was that the rules and regulations took a back seat to learning.

Sample Administrative Application

Depending upon our role in academic administration, some of us might claim that we have no power to share. We need to keep in mind, however, that as in the learner-centered classroom, even small gestures can make a big impact when it comes to offering people alternatives, a chance to share their views or opportunities for choice.

An administrative colleague of ours worked at an institution where the relationship between faculty and the administration was divisive, to say the least. The university had witnessed several work stoppages, and grievances abounded. Each time bargaining grew near, the same pattern of behavior would emerge: the faculty union would engage its crisis committee, and the administration would begin meeting regularly in what were ironically called "status continuance meetings." It was always clear that the two sides were headed for a battle and that the administration's goal was to maintain status quo. Even more ironic was the fact that the majority of the stakeholders in Academic Affairs never had any real input into the contract language by which they had to operate. This language was hammered out at the bargaining table under the supervision of an outside negotiator.

In an effort to share power, the year before the bargaining routine began, our colleague engaged two joint committees of administrators and faculty. The administrators included department heads and deans. The faculty association appointed bargaining unit members to take part. The committees were charged with developing language that both sides would like to see in the new contract. One committee focused on sabbatical leave, the other on post-tenure review.

The response to this fairly small gesture was remarkable. The faculty members were surprised to learn that many of the administrators were as frustrated by some of the language as they were. Both parties also quickly came to realize that they were in agreement in wanting processes of higher quality. Most important, however, was a new level of trust between the faculty and administration in Academic Affairs simply because they had been offered the opportunity to share power.

Function of Content: Prior Learning

The learner-centered paradigm is outcomes driven, so we don't talk about what we want to teach but rather what we want students to learn. In institutions governed by the instructional paradigm, it is not uncommon to find curricula designed around the particular interest of the professors in a unit rather than designed according to standard learning outcomes necessary for graduates. Course content according to what the professor is interested in rather than its relevance to student learning is a remnant of the instructional paradigm.

Learner-centered professors understand the role that prior learning plays in the students' ability to grasp new concepts. They recognize the importance of students' conceptual as well as cultural backgrounds and create learning environments that allow students to build upon what they already know and help students make connections and see the relevance of content as they construct their own knowledge.

Sample Teaching Practice

An example of using prior learning can be seen in Professor O's introduction to poetry course. Students generally don't like reading poetry. They find the syntax difficult, and they have been trained to believe that there is a hidden meaning that they can never understand without the professor translating for them. In an attempt to demystify the language of poetry, Professor O begins her class by having students read contemporary song lyrics. In the lyrics with which they are already familiar and readily understand, she points out the poetic elements that they will encounter in contemporary poetry. She also includes song lyrics that are difficult to understand and engages students in discussion of their interpretations of these lyrics. The students come to see that they already have a number of the skills needed to read poetry and that they are fairly adept at reading and understanding poetic language in the form of lyrics. This initial exercise creates a cognitive bridge for students. The next step, then, is for them to apply their prior knowledge to unfamiliar texts. Having established the fact that they indeed have prior knowledge makes the task simpler. They can approach lyric poetry of other eras with greater confidence and with a reference point or framework of understanding.

Function of Content: How Much to Cover

A second issue related to course content is how much to cover in a single course. Professors are feeling increasingly pressured to cover more content, particularly in fields where there is rapid acceleration of new knowledge, as in the sciences and technology. The instructional paradigm focuses on the transmission of knowledge, viewing the student as a receptacle into which teachers deposit knowledge, which Freire (2003) called the "banking theory" of teaching. The response to the rapid acceleration of knowledge in a field is for the professor to incorporate additional content. However, adding more courses or course content, transferring more information, will not transform students or adequately prepare graduates for the demands of the new workplace.

When we consider the function of content, we ask ourselves, What do my students have to know? rather than, What do I, as teacher, have to cover in the next fifteen weeks? Sometimes, covering less content can lead to deeper understanding of the fundamental concepts of a discipline, therefore providing better rewards and better learning or "deep learning," a concept derived from the work of Marton and Saljho (1976). Deep learning, as opposed to surface learning, relates previous knowledge to new knowledge, to knowledge from other courses, to knowledge of the real world, and organizes the knowledge into larger coherent structures. In other words, learning that is deep is learning that is integrated. The learner understands how the knowledge fits into the larger scheme.

Sample Teaching Practice

Professor D teaches an introductory course in the scientific method, a gateway course for new biology majors. As so often happens, whenever colleagues became frustrated with the shortcomings of students in their upper level biology courses, they saw adding content to the introductory course as the logical solution. Little by little, new content was added to the course along with an introduction to laboratory procedures, safety precautions, and on and on. The list of course outcomes had become so bloated that none of the topics could be adequately addressed. So Professor D and his two colleagues who also taught the course on a regular basis decided to reenvision the course. They began by surveying the department, asking a simple question of each colleague: "What knowledge and skills does a student have to be able to have mastered in order to learn in your course?"

They carefully phrased the question so that their colleagues had to consider what skills they built on in their own classes. The question asks about the conditions necessary for learning rather than feeding into the usual conversation about what they didn't have time to cover in their classes. The survey elicited interesting and surprisingly uniform responses. All indicated that knowledge of vocabulary of the field and practical application of the scientific method were essential. Some wanted specialized skills, but in the survey responses as a whole, there was unanimity about the necessary requirements.

Professor D and his colleagues redesigned the course around these core abilities, repeating them in various contexts, studying them more deeply. While no empirical study was conducted to monitor the change, anecdotally members of the department indicated that students entered the upper division courses with a sounder foundation and with more confidence in their abilities.

Learning Deeply and Broadly

Neuroscience has shown that the brain requires repeated practice in order to establish the pathways that become knowledge and that link old content to new. The learner-centered approach asks the teacher to think more holistically about course content, always focusing on the student outcomes, namely, what skills and abilities the student should be able to demonstrate by the end of the course and how the course's learning outcomes fit into the curriculum and meet the expectations for graduates from the institution.

Therefore, learner-centered teachers do not see course content as germane only to their courses but to other courses and to overall student learning outcomes. According to the American Psychological Association (2008), "Knowledge widens and deepens as students continue to build links between new information and experiences and their existing knowledge base. The nature of these links can take a variety of forms, such as adding to, modifying, or reorganizing existing knowledge or skills. . . . Unless new knowledge becomes integrated with the learner's prior knowledge and understanding, this new knowledge remains isolated, cannot be used more effectively in new tasks, and does not transfer readily to new situations" (para. 5).

If we take a look at some of the learning outcomes identified by the American Association of State College and Universities, we can see that these outcomes cannot be achieved by adding new courses. Students will not develop "habits of mind that foster integrative thinking and the ability to transfer skills and knowledge from one setting to another" (Crutcher, Obrien, Corigan, & Schneider, 2007,

p. 5) by adding course content, but this outcome can be achieved through learner-centered pedagogy applied across the curriculum. The same is true for "intercultural knowledge and collaborative problem-solving skills," and for excellent written and spoken communication. Instead of seeing the teaching of specific "knowledge" as the territory of specific departments, we begin to ask how these outcomes relate to individual disciplines and across disciplines. We begin to see institutional learning outcomes as the responsibility of all members of the institutional learning community. The Writing Across the Disciplines initiative faltered initially on many campuses because teaching writing was seen as the responsibility of the composition teacher, and other disciplines viewed the incorporation of writing into coursework as an add-on rather than a tool for learning the discipline. Because it is impossible in some disciplines to keep up with the acceleration of knowledge in the field, it becomes increasingly important for students in those disciplines to acquire the ability to learn on their own and to apply concepts across disciplines and to new learning situations.

The shift from the instructional paradigm to the learner-centered paradigm represents a shift away from content, transmission of knowledge, to a focus on learning: how can students construct their own knowledge and become self-consciously aware of how they learn? Psychological research has shown that successful learners develop thinking and learning strategies and that reflecting on how they learn can enhance learning, providing them with alternative strategies and optional methods for achieving learning outcomes (American Psychological Association, 2008). The institutional outcome is graduates who are lifelong learners who can readily adapt to new knowledge-environments, who are flexible and responsive to the rapidly changing demands of the twenty-first-century workforce.

Sample Administrative Practice

Because the instructional paradigm fosters a silo effect whereby individual departments, colleges, and divisions seem to operate independently from one another, when they communicate with one another they seem to be speaking different dialects, which results in miscommunication. Worse yet, between divisions, occasionally it seems as if completely different languages are being spoken. Cross-divisional teams create opportunities for individuals to learn about issues from multiple perspectives and, in the best instances, to begin to speak a common language.

An administrative colleague was assigned to a cross-divisional team charged with developing a computer hardware replacement schedule for the university. The members of the team included several academic deans, the associate vice president for Academic Affairs, the associate vice president for Student Affairs, and the supervisor of the IT Department as well as three IT unit coordinators. The initial meetings verged on comedy as the IT members listened to the academic deans discuss at considerable length why they didn't want new computers. It was evident that they were completely baffled by the deans' concerns. But after repeatedly meeting and coming to understand each others' concerns, all parties grew to respect the multiple challenges that this one issue presented to the different entities involved. The result was a hardware replacement program that all approved and an increased sense of cooperation among the divisional representatives.

The Role of the Teacher

Weimer (2002) provides a list of metaphors that have been used to describe the role of the learner-centered teacher: football coach (Barr & Tagg, 1995), midwife (Ayers, 1986), mountaineer (Hill, 1980), orchestra conductor (Eisner, 1983)—all of whom function as a guide. Currently the preferred metaphor is one provided by King (1993) in the catchphrase "from sage on the stage to guide on the side." All of these metaphors try to capture the essence of the learner-centered teacher as a facilitator of learning, one who helps others work and perform. Strategies that teachers use to accomplish this include problem-based learning, transformative learning, academic service learning, cognitive apprenticeship, and other active and reflective learning strategies. This approach is actually harder for everyone, student and teacher, because the teacher has to spend more time designing experiences that ultimately put the responsibility for learning—figuring things out, creating meaning—on the students who have been accustomed to having that done for them. It is important to recognize that students don't always like this either.

Sample Teaching Practice

A simple example of giving the responsibility for learning to the students comes from Professor J's courses in the College of Technology. In all his courses he provides a considerable amount of material for the students in the form of outside readings, study guides, specs for engine designs, as well as state and federal regulations. He refuses to organize all of this for the students. The students regularly complain, and he regularly replies that based upon what they already know about the subject, since many come in to the course with considerable practical experience, there is no single order to this information, that they have to read it and organize it for themselves as they understand and find it most useful. Rather than doing the learning for them, telling them how to understand, he requires them to organize the information according to their needs and prior knowledge.

Sample Administrative Practice

Teachers in the learner-centered paradigm spend more time designing experiences for students than telling them what they need to know. They also understand that it may take a longer time for learners to construct knowledge than to receive it, that telling may take less time but may not have the same long-term rewards. We both experienced this firsthand when we went through training to be Academic Quality Improvement Program (AQIP) peer reviewers for the Higher Learning Commission. The AQIP option for achieving accreditation through the Higher Learning Commission is based upon the Baldridge quality improvement model, and though the commission does not overtly express its aim in terms of a learner-centered paradigm, it is attempting to effect a shift in thinking within institutions toward the learner-centered paradigm. The AQIP review is formative, seeks to develop community both in the team reviewing and in the institution under review, and de-emphasizes the traditional power relationship in the old models of accreditation review, placing considerable emphasis on the context of the institution and its goals (taking into account the prior learning of the institution). The other feature that makes AQIP aligned with the learner-centered paradigm is that it is assessment driven.

The training for peer reviewers models learner-centered practices. The three-day training is divided into discussions with activities that foster team learning. In one of the early discussions each team is given a stack of cards with the pieces of the AQIP review process on each card. The instruction is for the team to discover the process of an AQIP review and create a visual representation. Because the AQIP system is highly individualized and organic in its structure, this task is much more difficult that it might appear. Each team ends up with a different visual representation, which reinforces for the trainees the individual nature of each review and the key role that context of the institution plays in the subsequent review process. While this information could have easily been disseminated in lecture, the activity required us to struggle with the nonlinear structure of the reviews and also to begin learning about achieving consensus as a team, which is key to the review process. The teachers in this training session designed this experience and then stepped aside while we engaged in the learning. They were always available to guide us, but for the most part, we were the ones responsible for the learning. And although it took us longer to figure this out for ourselves, we understood the concept deeply because we had to formulate and visualize and then articulate the knowledge rather than simply receive it via lecture.

Responsibility for Learning: Creating Community

As we noted previously, the responsibility for learning is shifted to the student in the learner-centered paradigm, but as Weimer (2002) so accurately describes, students are rarely prepared for this shift because they have become accustomed to extrinsic motivation through rules and regulations, policies to prompt their learning. She describes the climate for learning that fosters intrinsic motivation and student responsibility for learning. Earlier we stated that the metaphor for the instructional paradigm is a factory but the metaphor for the learner-centered paradigm is a community, a group of individuals who share a common goal or purpose and who through collaboration and teamwork establish authority, expertise, and responsibility for their learning. Fostering a sense of community is perhaps the most essential element both for learning in the classroom and for establishing the climate for a learning organization. Community is achieved through balancing power and control, creating a sense of relevance and connection, adopting practices that empower participants, and using assessment to monitor and motivate learning.

Creating community is not just about techniques used with students. It has everything to do with the professor's role in establishing and maintaining a climate conducive to learning. Specific strategies that teachers can adopt to create this climate for learning are presented in an assessment matrix in Chapter 5. Students are more receptive to performing when they believe that their professor genuinely cares about them and their learning. Caring about students' learning can be demonstrated in such simple ways as providing them with multiple means of contacting the professor and encouraging contact outside of class. Cranton (2004) defines "authenticity" in teaching as a multifaceted concept that includes being genuine, showing consistency between values and actions, relating to others in such a way as to encourage their authenticity, and living a critical life. Teachers who achieve this create challenging yet supportive conditions in which individuals work on authentic tasks. In analyzing the best practices of the best college teachers, Bain (2004) reported on years of research on college campuses studying the teaching of the very best teachers. He identifies key characteristics shared by these outstanding teachers, regardless of their discipline. Bain uses the word *trust* in describing the work of these individuals. Highly effective teachers tend to reflect a strong trust in students and display a willingness to share their own weaknesses.

In creating community, teachers pay attention to the social nature of learning because learning is social, and people learn through their interactions with each other and from each other. Through experiences such as group projects, peer review, and service learning, students are afforded the opportunity to observe other students learning and encourage and model those observations. By using tools that create authentic contexts for learning, teachers can optimize the potential for students to see relevance and meaning in the learning, thus encouraging motivation for learning.

Sample Teaching Practice

Year after year, Professor N is identified by seniors in the Honors Program as a professor who made the greatest impression of any professor during their years in college. Professor N is demanding, and her courses are considered rigorous, yet she is recognized over and over again for the care she gives to each student. At a banquet celebrating the graduating seniors, students give short presentations about the professor they identify as having made the greatest impression upon them. Each year that a student identifies Professor N, the student says the same things. Professor N knows each of her students by name and encourages students to come to her office and ask questions. She has strict rules but always explains that the rules are actually teaching them behaviors that nurses need to acquire. The students echo the same phrases in describing Professor N: "She is hard on us because she respects nursing and wants us to respect the

profession. She cares about how well we do and she cares about us as people." Professor N creates a climate for learning by demonstrating a respect for the discipline and esteem for the profession. The students want to be good enough to become part of this profession.

Sample Administrative Practice

Building community is perhaps the most important task for the learner-centered leader. Teachers build community by showing concern for the learning of their students, by making themselves accessible to their students, by creating relevance to learning situations and creating intrinsic motivation for learning. All three of these strategies are readily applicable to administrative work.

The instructional paradigm fosters competition and, as we discussed in an earlier example, a silo effect among colleges and divisions. A colleague of ours witnessed an example of this in the annual planning process at her institution. The process was inclusive and designed to gain participation at all levels. However, the implementation of the process had become highly competitive as each college would vie for resources by pandering to the presidential panel that viewed the presentations. Colleges literally sent spies to each other's presentations to see what gimmicks were employed, whether it was small children from the on-campus day care center singing to the president or refreshments that were known to be the president's favorites. Each year the presentations became more elaborate as colleges focused on grovelling for resources rather than genuine planning.

Under the leadership of our colleague, annual planning became a community event. Rather than having individual colleges make presentations to a presidential panel, the Division of Academic Affairs made one presentation that included all the colleges. Each dean was given a limit of two five-minute opportunities to speak, once on successes and again on plans for the future.

Because the planning was done as a community within the division rather than individual colleges working independently, there was cohesion to the presentation, and a theme emerged among the needs of the different colleges. Perhaps the most surprising result was that during the individual deans' presentations, each one, without prompting, made reference to work they were doing with other deans and colleges. By making annual planning a community project, rather than a competition, the division came together as a whole and discovered a shared vision.

Evaluation

At the exit interview of a program accreditation site visit, the accrediting reviewers offered some advice to the program faculty and staff. They suggested that more emphasis be given to the professional journals in the field and that students should learn more about their professional organizations. Defensively, the program coordinator quickly responded, "We teach that." The accreditation reviewer smiled patiently and responded, "But your students didn't learn it." This vignette illustrates the mode of thinking in the instructional paradigm. Just because professors present material does not assure that students learn it. In order to know whether students have learned, appropriate assessments and evaluation need to be employed. The program faculty and staff in our illustration did not understand the concept of assessment; the only assessment measures that they employed were student satisfaction ratings and grades.

Assessment and evaluation are key features of the learner-centered paradigm. We use *assessment* to refer to formative feedback and *evaluation* to refer to measurements of identified student learning outcomes. In the instructional paradigm, evaluation is summative, part of the competitive paradigm wherein tests sort the wheat from the chaff. In the learner-centered paradigm, evaluation and assessment are both summative and formative, used to gauge student progress as well as to monitor the effectiveness of teaching strategies.

In the learner-centered class, professors design various assessments in order to monitor the effectiveness of the designed learning strategies in the form of formative feedback mechanisms. A simple example is the lecture-response slip in which the professor asks students to answer one or two key questions related to the day's work. By reviewing the nongraded answers, the professor knows whether to review or forge ahead. The clicker response system is a high-tech version of feedback and proves especially valuable in large lecture sections in order to gauge student learning. Whether using lecture response slips, ungraded quizzes, individual conferences, class discussion, progress logs, journals, or some other technique, the purpose is for the professor to get feedback on whether learning is taking place.

Grades and Learning

Typically in the instructional paradigm, students are tested, perhaps only with a mid-term and a final, and assigned a grade, but the tests are not used as instructional tools. In some cases, students are not even allowed to see the test results, only the grade. This means of evaluation is in no way formative; it is, instead, a means of sorting students according to a single measure, timed test taking. In the instructional paradigm, where time is the constant and learning is the variable, this system makes sense. In the learner-centered paradigm, however, it does not. Testing is not a punishment or a trick of some sort. It becomes one means out of multiple measures to determine whether the learning we want to happen is, indeed, happening. Testing in the learner-centered paradigm is cumulative, for cumulative testing is one way of seeing whether deep learning is taking place, as opposed to surface learning, which fades from short-term memory.

Sample Teaching Practice

Professor P's sociology class offers an example of the mindset regarding testing in the learner-centered paradigm. Professor P was preparing his students for an exam. He took time at the end of class prior to the exam and began reading the test questions to the class. A student raised her hand and asked, "Are these like the questions that will be on the test?" He responded, "These *are* the questions that will be on the test." Another student raised her hand, looking rather perplexed and asked, "Why are you telling us the questions?" as though he had broken some cardinal law of teaching. He smiled and said, "Because I'd like you to know the answers."

The shift from the instructional paradigm to the learner-centered requires a shift in thinking about grades and what they mean in relation to learning. It is sometimes difficult for individuals to understand why grades are not measures of outcomes. The faculty members in our program under accreditation review at the opening of this section listed grades as an outcomes measure, stating that students must achieve a B in order to graduate from the program. In their heads they may have had a sense of the capabilities of the B student; however, they had no way of expressing what that B meant in relation to delineated student knowledge and abilities. Do all B students know the same materials or demonstrate the same skill levels? In looking at overall GPA, can a program coordinator claim that all students achieve a 3.0 in the same manner? Did some excel in some classes and not in others? Within an individual class, students who all take the same final exam and earn a 3.0 don't all miss the same questions. True outcomes measures are tied to specified learning outcomes, skills, and abilities that can be demonstrated by students.

Part of the vocabulary of the instructional paradigm is the label: A student, B student, C student. In using these terms to identify students, we deny the individuality of the learner. If asked to describe the B student, twenty professors might have some commonalities, but it is unlikely that the grade of C means the same to each. After all, students also rate professors according to the ease of their grading, which is one indication that they do not see all grades across courses as similar.

Sample Administrative Practice

The typical ways of establishing institutional accountability in the instructional paradigm are data driven but not quality driven. Institutions report six-year graduation rates and job placement rates as measures of success. While these are measures of success, they are not necessarily measures of student learning. Currently, because of the intense pressure placed on institutions to be accountable by the public and accrediting bodies, there has been a growing interest and awareness of the need for outcomes assessment. However, because we are still laboring under the influence of the instructional paradigm, assessment sometimes gets misconstrued. Rather than assessing because of the intrinsic motivation to see whether our students are learning, we end up responding to the extrinsic motivation of maintaining accreditation, jumping through hoops for external exigencies. Only when we become intrinsically motivated to know what learning is taking place will we develop a true culture of assessment.

Assessment can become a means of transforming culture. For example, if we return to the example we used at the outset of the chapter of the new faculty member who was deemed unprofessional by the tenure review committee for employing a pedagogical strategy that differed from the norm of the department, we can see how assessment could be used to resolve the disagreement. Rather than argue in the abstract about how students should be taught and the responsibility for holding students in the classroom for the designated amount of time, a more productive approach to resolving the conflict would be to treat the strategy as an experiment and assess for learning outcomes between courses taught with the traditional method and the alternative method. If students in both sections met the desired learning outcomes, then the concern over method becomes moot. Of course, if the students in the experimental section outperform the others, the results should foster a productive discussion of classroom methodology, spurring additional investigation.

Composition pedagogy witnessed this kind of cultural transformation thirty years ago. The traditional, logical method for teaching students how to write was to teach them grammar. For years, English professors had simply assumed that if they taught formal grammar, students would learn it and then their writing would improve. However, when researchers began testing this hypothesis, they found that the teaching of formal grammar had absolutely no effect in improving student writing; in fact, sometimes the reverse was true. Now, that isn't to say that there aren't still English teachers out there teaching formal grammar. As constructivist educational research has shown, there will always be those who refuse to accept evidence that challenges their long-held beliefs, but thirty years later, the majority of English teachers have revised their thinking about the place of formal grammar in a composition class. Assessment led to cultural change.

Concluding Thoughts

This chapter has provided only a first glance into the learner-centered classroom in order to serve as a point of reference and a metaphor for the model of leadership that we will propose for the learner-centered campus. Leading in the learner-centered paradigm has the promise of transforming academic leadership into the job we once envisioned academic leadership to be, one that fosters creativity and innovation in a community of scholars sharing a unified vision focused on learning and on the future.

Chapter Summary

The learner-centered classroom functions as the microcosm of the learner-centered institution. In other words, leaders can assume the role of teacher and guide their institutions toward learner-centeredness by applying the principles of learner-centeredness to the institution as a whole. The five main practices are the following:

- **Balance of power:** Creating community through sharing power and control

- **Function of content:** Creating relevance by focusing on what the learner learns as opposed to what the knowledge is to be disseminated

- **Role of the teacher:** Leaders assuming roles akin to the learner-centered teacher who is described as a facilitator, designer, or guide

- **Responsibility for learning:** Fostering a climate for learning by creating community

- **Assessment and evaluation:** Using assessment to monitor ongoing learning and gauge effectiveness.

Cultural transformation can be achieved through establishing a true culture of assessment and a community based on trust and empowerment.

4

Leading the New Paradigm
The Method for Change

In the previous chapters we described the instructional and learner-centered paradigms, contrasting the two so we get a better sense of where we are and where we want to be. As we have previously noted, the ability to see within one's current paradigm is a challenging task, and we will continue to use the metaphor of sight and vision as we discuss the skills necessary to bring about a shift to a new paradigm. The qualities of good leadership all involve seeing: (1) seeing the influence of the current paradigm, (2) seeing and visioning the future by realigning with the new paradigm, (3) seeing ways to model new behaviors, and (4) seeing the function of assessment and evaluation in reaching outcomes. In talking about shifting paradigms, the metaphor of the lens and the ability to see is a fundamental quality essential for making the transition from the old to the new. In this chapter we will examine the leadership skills necessary to lead institutions to the new paradigm.

In the previous chapter we made the point that the learner-centered classroom is a microcosm of the learner-centered institution and that administrators will adopt practices that are similar to those of the learner-centered teacher. Interestingly, if we examine current literature on leadership from the business realm, we will find that the advice for leaders is consistent with the learner-centered paradigm and correlates with the practices of learner-centered teachers. The traits that characterize the best leaders are the same traits that characterize the best teachers. To begin this chapter we would like to explore briefly this comparison between leading and teaching, for while academic leaders often enter their administrative roles with little formal leadership training or experience, most of them were successful teachers and as such have more experience to draw upon than they may realize.

Literature on Leadership

Leadership, as opposed to management, is the ability to move organizations from one point to another, to effect change, to set direction. Davis (2003) makes the distinction between leadership, promoting movement and change, and administration, sustaining an organization's mission. Similarly, Lick (2002) makes the point that management is about "doing things right"—in other words, working in a given paradigm to make things better. Leadership is about "doing the right thing," shifting a paradigm from "what is" to "what should be" (p. 32). Since our goal is to bring about the change from one paradigm to another, our focus will be on leadership. Literature on leadership focuses on the same principles that we identified as key characteristics of the learner-centered paradigm: sharing power, building community, and driving change through assessment and evaluation.

Sharing Power

Literature on leadership displays a trend moving away from traditional, hierarchical leading, sometimes referred to as the hero model of leading. Lucas (1994) describes the growth of the university hierarchy in the early twentieth century. He notes that as universities grew in size, the need for an infrastructure to manage the more complex organizations became apparent. The result was the hierarchical structure derived from business that is familiar to us today. While there was considerable resistance to the adoption of a business model for academia, Lucas (1994) notes that "not even the most ardent critics of business influence were prepared to advocate the elimination of bureaucracy entirely" for fear that without it the entire system would collapse (p. 193).

When we discuss the need for leaders to shift away from the hierarchical model of leadership, we are not suggesting that the hierarchy itself will disappear. After all, businesses that have adopted new leadership models have not dispensed with their corporate structures, though in many cases the hierarchy is significantly flattened. The issue is *how* one leads within the hierarchy, and here the analogy to the learner-centered classroom is illustrative. While learner-centered teachers may elect to share power and control, they are still in command of the class; it is their choice to share. As the designers of learning experiences, they are the responsible agents in fostering learning. The teacher is still the teacher but functions differently within this learning environment. Literature on leadership focuses on ways for leaders to function in less authoritarian ways within their organizations. Kotter (1996) writes, "Even today, the best performing firms I know that operate in highly competitive industries have executives who spend most of their time leading, not managing, and employees who are empowered with the authority to manage their work groups" (p. 167).

For the past twenty years the focus has been on leadership throughout organizations (Peterson, 1997; Kouzes & Posner, 2002, 2003; Senge, 1990), leading teams (Senge, 1990; Bensimon & Neumann, 1993; Lencioni, 2002; Hackman, 2002; Kouzes & Posner, 2002, 2003), leading as serving (Farnsworth, 2007; Greenleaf, 1977), and transformative leadership (Burns, 1978; Dolence & Norris, 1995; Traversi, 2007). This movement away from hierarchical leadership is closely aligned with the trend in education toward learner-centeredness, a movement away from hierarchy to community, from organizational systems to organizational cultures, a shift in focus from the leader as central figure and teacher as central figure to the empowerment of others within the community. While the sharing of power has been a major emphasis, we have not seen that shift in higher education. In fact, more and more we see challenges to shared governance as the ranks of tenured faculty shrink and the adjunct pools grow larger.

Building Community

Dolence & Norris (1995) use three similar metaphors to describe academic leadership in what they refer to as the emerging information age: "Administration in the 21st century university will assume the role of general contractor, developer and systems operator and auditor. These roles and responsibilities will require greater imagination than in the industrial age. As general contractor the academic administrator assures the necessary participants are working together" (p. 66). This concept is similar to Collins, in his popular *Good to Great* (2001), calling for leaders to get the right people on the bus. The developer, systems operator, and auditor are roles which involve design, requiring leaders to see that the proper resources are available and that outcomes are being met. The role is monitor and guide as opposed to heroic leader. Bensimon & Neumann (1993) similarly refer to leaders as less expert and more orchestrator (p. 2). Leaders in this model assume a role of supporter and designer, many of the very same metaphors used to describe the role of the teacher in the learner-centered paradigm in Chapter 3.

The concept of community is consistent with both the learner-centered paradigm and the literature on leadership. Dever (1997) writes in regard to leadership in learning organizations that "presidents and senior administrative staff need to be comfortable with fluid organizational dynamics that promote continuous learning, rigorous analysis and creative responses at all levels of the organization" (p. 62). Regardless of the terms used to describe leadership throughout the organization (for example, shared leadership, distributed leadership, multidimensional leadership, web of inclusion), the focus has shifted away from hierarchy to one of building relationships (Eddy & VanderLinden, 2006, p. 12). The fundamental qualities of successful leadership revolve around an understanding of the human condition. Covey (1989), Kotter (1996), and Kouzes and Posner (2002) all focus on the need for leadership to motivate and inspire others, for leaders to have vision and be able to articulate it. Gardner (1990) identified the cognitive attributes of leaders, noting that leaders stimulate change in others' behavior by telling stories and then emulating those stories in their own lives. Managers promote the status quo whereas leaders help others see the possibility for change and think differently about their world.

Consistent with the research of Kouzes and Posner (2002, 2003), who surveyed thousands of people regarding the qualities of great leaders, Gardner (1990) identified sharing a vision and modeling the way as the cognitive domain of leaders. In identifying the intelligences crucial to leaders, Gardner writes: "First, they are gifted in language; they can tell effective stories and often can write skillfully, too. Second, they display strong interpersonal skills; they understand the aspirations and fears of other persons, whom they can influence. Third, they have a good intrapersonal sense, a keen awareness of their own strengths, weaknesses, and goals, and they are prepared to reflect regularly on their personal course" (1990, p. 128).

Finally, the most effective leaders are able to address existential questions: They help audiences "understand their own life situations, clarify their goals, and feel engaged in a meaningful quest"(Gardner, 1999, p. 128). Gardner's description of the intelligences of leaders is not unlike Bain's (2004) description of the best teachers, that in addition to being passionate about their disciplines, they care about their students and student learning: "highly successful teachers have developed a series of attitudes, conceptions and practices that reflected well some key insights that have emerged from the scholarship on motivation" (p. 32). They understand how to foster intrinsic motivation in students, and they understand that learning can transform how one understands as well as what one understands. In short, great leaders and great teachers understand the human condition and how to motivate and inspire others.

Assessing the Context

We began Chapter 2 by illustrating the perceived disconnect between the description of academic leadership positions and the reality, positing that the reason is that the instructional paradigm forces administrators into the role of technician rather than leader. Like effective teachers, who resist the temptation to fix a student's work and instead focus on helping the student come to an understanding on his or her own, leaders need to resist the temptation to fix things for others and instead begin assessing the context by examining the existing knowledge, attitudes, and beliefs that underlie the current situation as an opportunity to learn and an opportunity to empower others to act.

In writing about process frontiers, which he defines as new areas of activity or modifications for organizations, organizational change theorist Peter Vaill (1996) warned against becoming obsessed by procedures and protocols that prevent individuals from having actual learning experiences. This obsession with how to do it is a technical approach to change, a hallmark of the instructional paradigm. Technical approaches to solving problems flourish in the instructional paradigm. Earlier we characterized this approach as one in which the administrator is the repairperson, replacing a part on a broken machine. Everyone understands what the solution or answer is and simply awaits implementation so that the machine will function once again.

Instead we call for an adaptive view, a wider and deeper approach requiring an examination of fundamental institutional values. Heifetz (1994) made the distinction between technical and adaptive work, technical work being basic problem-solving, and adaptive work being wider, more open-ended challenges that require innovation, consideration of values, and sometimes risk. Leading the way to the new paradigm will not be a technical exercise. Instead, it will be a learning experience for the individuals making the journey as well as for the institution as a whole. Leading the learner-centered campus will, above all, require mindfulness, self-awareness, focused avoidance of habitual behaviors, openness to new information, and an implicit awareness of more than one perspective.

Thinking of leading as *adaptive* is aligned with constructivist thinking regarding learning, which we discussed in Chapter 3. Piaget, from whose work constructivist theory is derived, described knowing as an adaptive activity. Von Glaserfeld (1995) explained that Piaget's conception of knowledge as adaptive is analogous to the concept of adaptation in evolutionary biology: "An animal that we call adapted has a sufficient repertoire of actions and states to cope with the difficulties presented by the environment in which it lives." (p. 7). In regard to cognition, humans also cope with difficulties on a conceptual level. Senge (1990) discussed leaders "seeking the truth" and observed that truth is not an absolute but an ongoing process of seeing the ways in which we deceive ourselves. Senge's statement is representative of what von Glaserfeld (1995) refers to as a shift to post-epistemological ways of thinking. Most important in this shift is the concept that *truth* as an absolute state of knowledge is replaced by *viability*, meaning that "to the constructivist, concepts, models, theories and so on are viable if they prove adequate in the contexts in which they were created. Viability—quite unlike truth—is relative to a context of goals and purposes" (p. 8).

Adaptive work, then, is about seeing and examining issues in a larger context in relation to the human condition. Rather than solving a problem by implementing a solution, the leader examines the context of the situation, considers broader implications of multiple solutions and perspectives as well as whether the system should be changed or modified rather than repaired or fixed. More importantly, the leader is not the problem solver but encourages and empowers others to take actions that will resolve the issue.

This adaptive approach is consistent with strategies of learner-centered teaching. An adaptive approach to problem-solving requires leaders to take a broader view of the issues and to study the values of the individuals or institutions that underpin the situation (Harris & Cullen, 2007). They must learn to diagnose problems in light of the human dimension, the values involved, multiple perceptions of the problem, recognizing that issues may be threatening to individuals because they threaten established values or ways of working. Similarly, leaders must empower others to act, thus requiring trust. In leading the learner-centered campus, we need to resist the temptation to fix things for others, to simply explain the error of their ways, and instead, begin by examining the existing knowledge, attitudes, and beliefs that underlie the current situation, using each situation as an opportunity to learn and an opportunity to empower others to act. By approaching problem solving from an adaptive view, leaders gain insight to the current reality. They see the issue within the context of the paradigm that governs it, and they also see issues in relation to the human dimension, the social norms and attitudes that created it.

Four-Step Strategy for Change

We believe that a comprehensive approach to shifting toward learner-centeredness is essential, an approach that will involve all members of the institution applying this four-step process within their spheres of influence. These four steps are comparable to the best practices of classroom teaching. Good teaching calls for assessing the current knowledge, attitudes, and understanding of one's students. Teachers need to know what their students know in order to help them reach learning outcomes. They set measurable learning outcomes which serve as a goal for learners as well as a means of monitoring progress. They regularly assess progress, and finally they model the best behaviors of scholarship and learning. The same is true for leading.

> **Step One:** We need to learn to see our current reality in relation to the instructional paradigm and begin to assess every process in light of the current paradigm. What is our state of affairs and to what extent does the instructional paradigm govern it?

Step Two: We need to ask ourselves how current processes can be redesigned or even eliminated, in order to realign with the new paradigm. We set goals, a process that grows out of the new paradigm.

Step Three: We need to consider how assessment and evaluation can be infused into the process so that they become the drivers for cultural change. As Kouzes and Posner (2002) so aptly stated, "What gets measured, gets done" (p. 82).

Step Four: We need to model a learner-centered approach. As Gardner (1990) described in talking about the intelligences of leaders, they tell stories to illustrate the vision and then emulate those stories in their own lives.

Step One: Seeing the Current Paradigm

Farnsworth (2007) describes higher education's apparent inability to adapt, highlighting a variety of forces that are impediments to change, among them the intellectualism of the academy, what he sees as the academy's stance as repository of knowledge, the power wielded by academic discipline, and professional protections that provide veto power to those for whom change is threatening. We have noted many of the same forces, as have others before us. Farnsworth's solution is for leadership to learn to listen, making time to listen, hearing what is really being said, and learning to listen critically. While we would never discount the value of listening, we will argue that before listening, one must learn to see and help others to see. If we simply listen to the voices within the instructional paradigm, we will not hear anything new.

Farnsworth suggests that the combination of the tenure system, professional rank, faculty associations and unions, as well as shared governance has created a sense of invulnerability among those who refuse to change. We would argue that those who appear to have a vested interest in impeding change do not solely reside in faculty ranks, nor do they resist change because of vested interest or even a conscious effort to thwart change, but instead do so because their vision is regulated by the instructional paradigm. The need for protectionism grew out of that paradigm. Until we learn to see the construct that is binding our thinking and our behavior, we will, of course, protect ourselves. It is only natural that individuals will protect what they have if they have nothing else to choose from, no better place to go. Seeing is the first step to addressing this very natural, human response. We need to see the reality of our current situation and then see the vision of where we could be before we will be able to change. We must learn to see in order to adapt.

Senge (1990) wrote about seeing and speaking the truth. He referred to it as "a simple yet profound strategy . . . [B]eing committed to the truth is far more powerful than any technique" (p. 148). Seeing the truth, the kind of honesty that Senge refers to, is difficult to achieve but it is exactly the kind of honesty that is needed if we are to shift into a new paradigm. Senge is referring to the *myths* that we tell ourselves as institutions. He clarifies what he means by seeking the truth this way: "Commitment to the truth does not mean seeking the Truth, the absolute final word or ultimate cause. Rather, it means a relentless willingness to root out the ways we limit or deceive ourselves from seeing what is, and to continually challenge our theories of why things are the way they are" (p. 148). In other words, seeing the truth is about learning to see the paradigm in which we operate, questioning habits of mind.

Habitual Blindness

Part of the *habit* of the traditional paradigm is that we begin to believe the myths we tell ourselves. Bits of our institutional history become part of our institutional identity, and no one is comfortable in having his or her identity challenged. This leads to habitual blindness, accepting what we believe to be true without examination or intentional analysis. In talking about transformation, Mezirow (2000) referred to habits of mind as the "web of assumptions and expectations through which we filter the way we see the world" (p. 22). These are habitual, implicit rules for interpreting experience. Leaders to and of the new paradigm will be called upon to be mindful of these habitual rules, to question them, and in many cases to change them. Through this we aspire to create institutions that are more inclusive and community oriented, led by individuals who are discriminating and intentional in their thought and action.

For example, the faculty and staff at Friendly State University (FSU) believe that one of their identifying characteristics as an institution is their friendliness toward students. When asked by marketing consultants what makes FSU different from competitors, the refrain is "We're student friendly." When developing a strategic plan, the refrain appears again, "We're student friendly."

However, the learner-centered leader who seeks the truth and relies on assessment to drive change, asks the question, "If we're so friendly to students, why are more students transferring out than transferring into the institution?" The members of the university community do not want to consider this possibility. They question that data and claim that the numbers are not accurate. They insist that if the numbers are true, that it is an anomaly. Instead of investigating the "anomaly," they question the administrator's motives in bringing this issue forward. This is the kind of truth seeking that Senge is referring to. It is easier and more comforting to believe the myth that we are student friendly than it is to honestly deal with the possibility that our policies and practices may not be all that friendly after all. Even if leadership does recognize the problem, it is easier to allow people to believe that they are doing well, that they are perceived as friendly, than it is to confront a reality that challenges longstanding beliefs.

Senge (1990) writes that the power of truth is in learning to see reality more and more as it is, "cleansing the lens of perception, awakening from self-imposed distortions of reality" (p. 150). And that is the kind of honesty it will take to shift the paradigm. Honesty is about seeing, and the lens metaphor is again useful. Glass is meant to be seen through. When we wash a window or clean our eyeglasses, we learn to focus on the glass. We see in a way that is not our normal way of seeing. We learn to see the surface of the glass that under normal, everyday, *habitual* circumstances, we see through. Once we learn to see in this new way, to see the surface of the glass, we begin to notice imperfections; we see what we had trained ourselves to ignore. We need to learn to see the surface of the glass of the instructional paradigm in order to identify the imperfections and act upon them. This is the first and most important step in leading to the new paradigm.

Step Two: Realigning with the New Paradigm

The second kind of vision that leaders need is a vision of the future, in this case, envisioning what our institutions, our policies, our behaviors will be in the new paradigm. Kouzes and Posner's (2002) extensive research on what people look for most in leaders identified *forward thinking* at the top of the list. People want leaders who have a vision for the future and who can see where they need to go. What Kouzes and Posner are really talking about is leadership with a vision and plan for the future, leadership with direction. Vision for the future requires more than simply setting a target for enrollment or establishing fundraising objectives. Vision is also different from mission. Pielstick (1997) writes that mission is defining what the business of the institution is whereas vision defines the *behavior* and in this way organizational culture and vision interact with one another. He clarifies, "Several characteristics are ascribed shared vision. It provides meaning for the employees and other stakeholders. It inspires and often excites, motivating individuals to extra effort to achieve the vision. The shared nature of the vision is unifying, creating a sense of community" (p. 21).

Shared vision is critical for it provides the goal, the place we are moving to, which is essential if people are going to be willing to leave behind where they were. If we make an analogy to the learner-centered classroom, the shared vision is equivalent to the learning outcomes for the institution. The vision is what we are trying to achieve, and like good learning outcomes, the vision should be measurable and assessable. In talking about vision, Kotter (1996) writes, "Vision plays a key role in producing useful change by helping to direct, align, and inspire actions on the part of large numbers of people. Without an appropriate vision, a transformation effort can easily dissolve into a list of confusing, incompatible and time-consuming projects " (p. 7).

Inspiration Through Engagement

Inspiration is all about engaging others. Kotter (1996) writes that "Leadership defines what the future should look like, aligns people with that vision and inspires them to make it happen despite the obstacles" (p. 25). People respond to optimism. They need hope. Fear is a debilitating force, whether it is in the classroom or in the organization, immobilizing rather than mobilizing, inhibiting individuals' ability to learn. People perform their best, whether they are students in a classroom or employees in an organization, when they feel safe, have trust in their community, and feel empowered. Creating this environment involves risk but also requires development for just as students in classrooms need to learn how to exercise power, the same is true for all members of the institution who have not previously been empowered. Kotter (1996) notes that "Many of the same kinds of organizational attributes required to develop leadership are also needed to empower employees. Those facilitating factors would include flatter hierarchies, less bureaucracy, and greater willingness to take risks" (p. 167). Empowerment, ownership, and investment are key to success.

How institutions begin this assessment of policies and practices will be highly individualized. All policies need to be realigned, however. The shift to a learner-centered paradigm is not isolated to the classroom nor is it isolated to academic affairs. The shift involves the entire campus.

The Importance of Failure

As we lead the way into the new paradigm, we will need to find ways to demonstrate the working habits of the new paradigm, to model the way. We will need to model the desire to learn, the willingness to make mistakes, the ability to work in teams, the willingness to share power and control, the willingness to trust others, the reliance on assessment and evaluation, and the willingness to experiment.

Leaders in the learner-centered paradigm believe that intelligence is expandable, believe in lifelong learning and that everyone continues to learn and to make mistakes, not just students. Because of the intensely competitive nature of the instructional paradigm, too many times in academe we adopt what Dweck (2006) would call a fixed mindset and spend the greater part of our time validating that we are as smart as we are believed to be. Making mistakes is not something that academics tend to accept readily. Mistakes are seen as flawed intellect rather than a means to grow and learn. Covington (1992) notes that failure is tied to learning and success: "Failure is interesting in part for the fact that successful thinkers actually make more mistakes than those who give up easily and therefore preserve their unblemished record of mediocrity and also for the fact that mistakes can usually be set right by trying again" (p. 231). The result of this attitude is an unwillingness to take risks, to experiment. Business theorist Chris Argyris (1993) labeled this behavior "skilled incompetence" (para. 1), the psychological need of individuals to protect themselves from appearing ignorant. Senge (1990) writes about this phenomenon: "School trains us never to admit that we do not know the answer and most corporations reinforce that lesson by rewarding people who excel in advocating their views, not inquiring into complex issues. Even if we feel uncertain or ignorant, we learn to protect ourselves from the pain of appearing uncertain or ignorant. That very process blocks out any new understanding which might threaten us. The consequence is 'skilled incompetence'—teams full of people proficient at keeping themselves from learning" (p. 26).

As leaders in the learner-centered paradigm, we must create an atmosphere of trust and one that is forgiving of error in order to foster an environment that is flexible and supportive of experimentation. Brookfield (2006) noted that it is essential for those in leadership positions to talk publicly about their mistakes and to continue to learn from them: "Certainly, junior members of any organizational work team will usually never dream of admitting a mistake unless and until the team's leader, as well as other senior figures of the organization, repeatedly admit to their mistakes and disclose how these are triggers to beneficial new learning. This needs to be a valued organization-wide practice" (p. 837).

Experimenting with an Adaptive Approach

An administrative colleague of ours was challenged with an international program that was experiencing a decreasing population and the growing isolation of the few international students on campus. The program had been without a director for several years while the previous administration had wrestled with the problem. The structure of the existing program was insular. The director was a half-time recruiter for international students while simultaneously serving as the on-campus coordinator of international activities and services. The international students were oriented through the Office of International Affairs (OIA), and sought academic support there as well as necessary support with visas and residential issues. Because so many of the services as well as social opportunities were conducted through the OIA, students gravitated to that office but did not become fully integrated into the larger campus community.

As an opportunity to model his belief in experimentation, our colleague decided to try out a new model, restructuring the international student services based upon the Harvard model of inclusion, which meant that the OIA, as it had previously operated, was eliminated. The goal was to mainstream international students, providing the same support services but doing so through the existing campus infrastructure. Therefore, instead of having international students recruited by one individual working out of Academic Affairs, recruiting of international students was conducted through the Office of Admissions and Recruitment. Instead of providing separate academic support services for international students through the OIA, academic support was conducted through the Writing Center and Academic Skills Center, the campus academic support services used by all students. The position of international student advisor was retained; however, rather than locating that individual in the OIA, the advisor was added to the staff of support personnel in the campus advising services unit.

The resulting clamor over this decision is illustrative of the resistance people have to experimentation within the instructional paradigm as well as the expectations that individuals have for technical problem solving. For months, individuals from various areas on campus had been up in arms that nothing had been done about the OIA. They demanded that action be taken. However, they were expecting a technical solution. They expected that another director would be hired and that the "machine" would be fixed and everything would go back to normal. The approach that our colleague took was not well received. The same individuals who had been demanding for our colleague to take action were now up in arms because he had not simply replaced parts in the existing system; instead, he eliminated the machine in favor of a new model. The notion of experimentation within the instructional paradigm is often met by fear and suspicion, and this was the case with this experiment. People were concerned that international students would be lost, that they would not know how to maneuver on a small rural campus though the majority of them came from large, urban centers overseas. Our colleague was accused of being hostile to international students in spite of the fact that he had firsthand knowledge, having experienced the transition to the United States as an international student himself. To the many distressed inquiries of "What if it doesn't work?" he responded, "Then we'll try something else."

In modeling the habits of the learner-centered paradigm, we need to foster experimentation and innovation. Likewise, we need to assess our experiments and recognize when further innovation is required. And we need to be prepared for resistance, for just as students are often resistant to the responsibility for learning that is shifted to them in the learner-centered classroom, members of the larger institution will be resistant to change as well.

Step Three: Assessing

MacTaggart (2007) describes the autocrat who abhors shared governance as demanding, manipulative, and insistent on making all decisions. This leadership style is not the one that characterizes those who have successfully transformed institutions. Instead, it is the collaborative leader who is unafraid of assessment, an accomplished communicator and consensus builder who attains buy-in for a shared vision, who has the most success in these critical situations of transforming failing institutions. Being unafraid of assessment and evaluation is key, for those leaders understand that assessment and evaluation are integral components for driving change and meeting challenges. Because we are still laboring under the influence of the instructional paradigm, we can sometimes lose our focus on the motivation for assessment.

One of the indicators that the motivation for assessment is extrinsic rather than intrinsic is when the assessment loop has not been completed, in other words, when institutions conduct assessment and review the data but stop at that point without taking action. Based upon the continuing focus on "closing the loop" at conferences like the Annual Assessment Institute sponsored by IUPUI and in training sessions for accrediting agency peer review teams, the phenomenon of not closing the loop is evidently still pervasive.

If we are intrinsically motivated to assess, we are genuinely interested in knowing whether what we are assessing is having an effect, ideally the intended effect. We do so in order to modify and improve our processes. Collecting and analyzing data but never taking action suggests that our motivation is not to make changes and modifications, but instead to validate that what we are doing is already good; institutionally we are exhibiting a "fixed mindset" as described earlier in relation to the importance of error. Admitting weakness is a threat to our identity. When we introduced the underlying values of the instructional paradigm, we discussed how in a paradigm that values control, individuals focus on pleasing the boss or the teacher rather than developing intrinsic motivation to learn. Collecting assessment data without completing the feedback loop is akin to the student in the instructional paradigm trying to please the teacher rather than genuinely trying to learn. In this case, institutions are trying to please accrediting bodies or other outside agencies because of the control those bodies hold over them. Another way of looking at this is to think about the use of grading in the instructional paradigm. Grades are not assessment tools since they do not give feedback on specific outcomes. They are, instead, a means of labelling and codifying. This desire to grade and codify has been the driving force behind the Spellings Commission and other governmental regulatory bodies that want what they call accountability. This mindset is indicative of the stranglehold the instructional paradigm has on our mode of thinking. In sum, the fact that we are conducting assessment is not an indication that we have shifted to a learner-centered paradigm or that we have created a culture of assessment.

Assessment efforts have faltered on many campuses because the focus has been on outcomes rather than on learning. Assessment is tied to "seeing the truth," and it is incumbent upon leadership to create an atmosphere of trust whereby seeing the truth outweighs the fear of poor results and/or reprisal. Only in a learning-centered environment will assessment truly work because individuals must feel secure enough to be honest about the results.

As we work toward creating a true culture of assessment, we should consider the types of assessments we currently employ and examine them in light of the values of the instructional paradigm. A comparison of two methods of assessing writing illustrates this concept. At one time, timed pre- and post-course impromptu writing samples were widely employed to determine growth in writing ability of students in composition courses. Often, the rubrics used to assess these pieces of writing were the same rubrics used for placing students in various levels of writing courses in spite of the fact that rubrics for placement generally target gross features related to audience, organization, development, and editing, whereas rubrics designed to gauge growth in writing ability over a short period, ten or fifteen weeks, need to be far more sensitive to subtle signs of maturation. It was no wonder, then, that trying to measure growth over ten or fifteen weeks using rubrics that focused on gross features more often than not showed that little or no growth had occurred. A common analogy for this practice is gauging one's weight loss using a truck scale. The mechanism for assessment is not properly aligned with the purpose for the assessment.

For a variety of reasons, this practice has largely fallen out of use in part because the testing method was not in alignment with the pedagogical goals including such skills as revision. It is interesting, though, to consider why this method of assessment was chosen in the first place since in reality, individuals are rarely asked to sit down and compose an impromptu essay. Even if the argument were made that students need this skill for writing essay exams in other courses, the truth is that in the case of an examination in a subject area, the student would have a fair idea of the topics prior to writing. The design of this assessment practice clearly grows out of the mindset of the instructional paradigm. In fact, the design specifications were predicated upon a notion of a "controlled" testing situation. The pre- and post-test design as well as the time limit for writing emerge from a paradigm in which, as Tagg (2003) articulated, time is the constant and learning is the variable. The insistence that the topic be impromptu is indicative of a lack of trust in students. Because they might prepare ahead of time, in other words, they might think about the subject; they need to be surprised by the topic because we wouldn't want to encourage thinking outside of the time designated for the test. This model devalues the individual, in this case, the individual differences among writers and their composing processes, and is focused on labelling rather than learning.

The portfolio method of assessment has grown in popularity over the past years. It is a method which is much more closely aligned with the values of the learner-centered paradigm. The portfolio assessment looks at a collection of works produced by the student over a period of time. In selective portfolios, students choose which pieces they want to represent their work; in other cases, the portfolios are comprehensive, representing all work including drafts and prewriting. Unlike the pre-post, timed, impromptu writing assessment, the outcomes—in this case, the finished written pieces—become the focal point rather than the controlled situation in which the writing was produced. The portfolio method accounts for individual differences in composing behaviors. This method also displays more trust in the individual and in cases where the student is allowed to select the pieces for evaluation, the method is empowering, allowing for student input and control.

The focus on assessment and evaluation in the learner-centered paradigm will reflect the values of that paradigm, namely learning. The learner-centered paradigm is truly a culture of assessment. We will conduct assessments because we truly want to learn, change, grow, improve, not because we are meeting the demands of some external body that holds power over us. In the learner-centered paradigm, assessment and evaluation drives quality improvement because assessment is tied to outcomes and goals, and in the larger sense tied to the shared vision for the institution.

In our discussion of the instructional paradigm, we said that it was driven by policy and precedent. When individuals make decisions in an organization governed by the instructional paradigm, their first impulse is to find the policy. The learner-centered paradigm is outcomes driven, so when individuals make decisions in this paradigm, their first impulse is to examine the assessment results. Using assessment as the tool to guide decision making is one means of creating a culture of assessment.

Step Four: Modeling a Learner-Centered Approach

Leading the learner-centered campus will, above all, call upon leaders to be learners—to learn to see how the instructional paradigm governs their operations; to learn how to realign operations to be consistent with the values of the learner-centered paradigm; to learn how to model the way in order to make the shift visible, understandable, and credible; and to learn how to infuse assessment and evaluation throughout the organization to act as a measurable driver of change. Reflection is key to developing the ability to do this, reflection that is ongoing and critical.

We have made the analogy between learning to operate in the new paradigm and learning to speak a new language. In learning a new language, practice is essential. Our point is that leaders as learners must take part in activities that foster their learning, that give them opportunities to practice operating within the new paradigm. Two critical learning tools, consistent with research on learning, are (1) self-reflection through writing and (2) collaborative learning through discussion with others. Leaders need to practice speaking in the new paradigm in order to achieve automaticity, to develop new habits of mind.

The Leadership Portfolio

One practice that offers this opportunity is the leadership portfolio. We recommend that leaders develop a portfolio as a vehicle for monitoring and documenting their progress, a method that incorporates both critical reflection and collaboration. Recall Gardner's description of the cognitive domain of leaders who reflect regularly on their personal course. The leadership portfolio is a tool to help leaders do just that.

Portfolios are widely used as tools for assessment of student learning and as evidence of professionals' competency and range of skills and talents. Probably what first comes to mind when we think of professional portfolios is the artist's portfolio that illustrates style, growth, development, thematic interests, and stylistic influences. Faculty members have long used portfolios in this way to demonstrate competency for tenure and promotion. The use of the portfolio is becoming more common among academic administrators, especially in the K–12 arena. Sabin (2007) describes the use of the portfolio by superintendents as a means of demonstrating evidence of their worth both to superiors and to the public. The portfolio he describes is reflective rather than comprehensive, illustrating the individual's growth both in skills and effectiveness. Most important, the process serves as "an authentic way to stimulate and document professional growth" (p. 3).

The Portfolio's Goals

The leadership portfolio provides leaders a mechanism for meeting several leadership goals key to shifting the paradigm: establishing community and trust, articulating vision and goals, modeling the way, and assessing processes. First, making the document accessible to faculty and staff can serve as a dramatic gesture of trust and cooperation, perhaps one of the hardest goals to achieve in the process of moving away from the instructional paradigm. Second, the portfolio provides a learning opportunity for leaders in terms of self-reflection and analysis and it gives faculty insight into the work by leadership on behalf of student learning, providing transparency to the process. Third, it is emblematic of our role as learners, working to continuously improve our performance and achieve goals and outcomes; it provides leaders with an opportunity to model the way. Fourth, it serves as a record of accomplishments, an assessment document that records the goals met as well as the challenges yet to be addressed. Developing a leadership portfolio that is open to review by the institutional community provides an excellent opportunity for the type of reflection needed to lead the learner-centered campus. A portfolio developed through critical reflection and collaboration is both an excellent method for practicing thinking in the new paradigm and has the potential for becoming an artifact of great significance.

What to Include

Seldin and Higgerson (2002) provide practical advice for developing an administrative portfolio. In line with the values of the learner-centered paradigm, the model they suggest is creative, supported by documentation, and collaborative. They recommend that the individual creating the portfolio consider himself or herself as an artist or designer, creating a thematic approach to the presentation of his or her best work. Also in keeping with the best practices of leadership, they suggest that it be biographical as well as thematic, that the portfolio tell a story. They see collaboration as one of the defining features of the administrative portfolio, for through collaboration and mentoring, the designer of the portfolio has a richer opportunity for reflection and self-awareness.

The portfolio they describe begins with a one-page introductory statement of the purpose and context of the individual's work. This is followed by two or three pages with the individual's job description and responsibilities as well as a reflective statement of his or her administrative philosophy, objectives, and strategies. This section also includes performance evaluations from multiple sources. The remaining sections focus on innovations, special projects with evidence of impact, and significant accomplishments as well as goals.

We recommend developing the administrative portfolio to reflect the values of the learner-centered paradigm by specifically focusing on the qualities that characterize good teaching and leading. For example, Seldin and Higgerson (2002) suggest that the opening statement provide the purpose and context of the individual's work. Context is key to learning in the learner-centered paradigm. Teachers understand that each learner brings a different context to the learning opportunity. The same is true of leaders as learners. The statement of context should not only reflect on the contextual features of the individual's position within the institution but also examine the attitudes, beliefs, and experiences that the person brings to the position and to the challenge. In fostering a community of trust, as we noted, leaders must be willing to share their own weaknesses or mistakes. The portfolio provides a wonderful opportunity to do this, particularly in the opening contextual statement. One might begin by asking, How have I been shaped by the instructional paradigm? What habits will be the most difficult to change? Recognizing that my greatest asset is also my greatest liability, what will be my greatest challenge? Answering these three questions offers opportunities to provide biographical information, to tell stories.

We want to clarify what we mean by "autobiographical statement" so that readers don't toss the book aside at this point, thinking, "These people are nuts. I'm not revealing my weaknesses to my colleagues in a public document!" The reflection that we have in mind is in regard to leadership traits and how they may have been informed by the instructional paradigm. The audience for the portfolio is not a therapist but colleagues who will also be considering the same questions. So, rather than examining our anxiety about being confined in small spaces or our inability to eat food wrapped in cellophane, we're thinking more about traits that we have developed because of the power of the instructional paradigm, the paradigm we already have success in working within.

For example, the instructional paradigm values technical problem solving. Many of us are extremely adept at this and have seen it as a strength because we have kept our machine running smoothly, preventing "problems" from rising to the next level within the hierarchy. In the learner-centered paradigm, this strength becomes a liability, for the learner-centered paradigm asks leaders to empower others, asks them not to rush in and fix the problem so it goes away but to step back and analyze it and then empower others to learn how to resolve it. The challenge for some individuals will be to resist fixing things, in part because we have already had success by using that approach and also because that approach has become a habit.

Resisting the temptation to be a technician may prove to be the most difficult habit to change because of the personal risk involved. Even though we are not revealing personal idiosyncrasies and anxieties in the leadership portfolio, when we adopt the role of learner, we are adopting a position that is counter to the most basic nature of operators in the instructional paradigm: being the authority figure. Just as the teacher in the learner-centered classroom assumes risk by relinquishing the role of sage and holder of all knowledge, the leader who has the courage to adopt the role of learner becomes vulnerable to those still operating in the instructional paradigm, who define themselves by their position of knowing. We have all witnessed academic interchanges that are nothing more than intellectual jousting, jockeying with one another for the honor of smartest individual in the room. One colleague of ours who is particularly immersed in this intellectual competitive mindset begins each sentence of an exchange of dialogue with "I know that." Other colleagues joke that "I know that" is his middle name. Changing this cultural attitude will be a tremendous challenge.

While it may run counter to our survival instincts and to our basic human impulses to knowingly assume a position of vulnerability, in fact, taking that risk can disarm those whom we might expect would take advantage. Vulnerability enhances trust. Recall that in transformative teaching strategies, the disorienting strategy is the catalyst for learning. The leader who assumes the personal risk of assuming the role of learner, the leader who doesn't have all the answers ready and waiting to be applied, can be very disorienting. While not a perfect analogy, it is similar to the person who responds to a verbal attack with a simple "I'm sorry" rather than going on the defensive, thus totally disarming the attacker because the response was counterintuitive.

Practicing strategies that are counterintuitive eventually alters what is intuitive. Take for example, learning to ski. When we are taught to ski the instructor tells us to lean forward toward the bottom of the ski slope. This act is counter to our natural inclination to lean sideways with the ground. Eventually, through repeated practice, as we become more expert in our skiing, leaning forward becomes automatic, becomes intuitive. Although the portfolio serves several purposes, the practice it provides in developing automaticity of thinking within the new paradigm, of altering what is intuitive for us, is perhaps the most critical reason for engaging in the activity.

Critical Reflection

Brookfield (1995) provides a rich and methodical approach to critical reflection. As he so aptly notes, "attempting to become aware of our assumptions is a puzzling and contradictory task" that very few can do on their own (p. 28). For that reason, he recommends four "lenses" to aid teachers in the process of self-reflection: autobiographies as learners and teachers, our students' eyes, our colleagues' experiences, and theoretical literature. These same four lenses, with slight modification, can be applied to self-reflection for academic leaders.

We have already mentioned the use of autobiography, the first lens. Brookfield (1995) explains that autobiography plays an important role in creating community: "The fact that people recognize aspects of their own individual experiences in the stories of others is one reason for the success of peer support groups for those in crisis or transition.... As we talk to each other about critical events in our practices, we start to realize that individual crises are collectively experienced dilemmas" (p. 31). Analyzing our autobiographies can often help us pinpoint why certain practices are favored, for example. Cranton (2004) talks about "authenticity" in teaching: "Authenticity is a multi-faceted concept that includes at least four parts: being genuine, showing consistency between values and actions, relating to others in such a way as to encourage their authenticity, and living a critical life" (p. 7). Authenticity in leadership calls for the same qualities, as has been noted by various experts on leadership discussed in Chapter 3.

The second lens for critical reflection of leadership would be the eyes of those we serve, faculty and staff. Gaining the perceptions of faculty and staff provides necessary feedback as well as a reality check. Are we indeed walking our talk? Do faculty and staff feel empowered? Is there a growing sense of community and engagement? Just as providing anonymity to students gains honest responses, faculty and staff must also have anonymity if the feedback is to be genuine.

The third lens for reflection is colleague perception. Along with the added perspective, Brookfield (1995) notes that colleague feedback can also provide needed sustenance, as he writes, "We start to see that what we thought were unique problems and idiosyncratic failings are shared by many others who work in situations like ours. Just knowing that we're not alone in our struggles is profoundly reassuring" (p. 36). Collegiality and mentoring among academic leaders are essential if we are to hold true to the new paradigm, and here we would emphasize that this collegiality extends beyond academics. It is critical that all leadership throughout the institution work together to understand the new paradigm and to realign practices and processes.

Brookfield (1995) explains the concept of collaborative problem solving in relation to teaching. The process is easily adapted to academic leadership. He calls it the Good Practice Audit (GPA), and it involves three stages: (1) problem formation, (2) individual and collective analysis of experience, and (3) compilation of suggestions for practice (p. 162). Collaboratively, colleagues define a problem, share experiences with the identified problem, and develop a list of possible actions for solution.

The fourth lens is theoretical literature. Literature leading to the new paradigm would include literature on learning as well as literature on leadership. One of the by-products of becoming critically reflective, according to Brookfield (1995), is that we become authentic and consistent. Consistency is essential and can be achieved by continuously reflecting on literature on learning, deepening our understanding.

Developing a leadership portfolio is a self-reflective process that embraces the basic values of the learner-centered paradigm, for it is centered on the individual's self-awareness of learning; it is a collaborative activity that requires assessment and evaluation, encourages reflection from multiple perspectives, and takes into account the context of experiences that the individual brings to the challenge. Furthermore, the process of developing it is itself a learning experience. The finished product (which is never really finished, for critical reflection is ongoing) articulates a vision and has the potential to illustrate the expansive vision of the best leaders. Recall the four types of vision that leaders need: vision for the current reality (in this case, the ability to see the instructional paradigm) vision for the reality that can be (in this case, understanding of the learner-centered paradigm), vision within oneself (demonstrated through critical reflection of one's self both as a product of the instructional paradigm and a pioneer leading the way to the new paradigm), and vision within others in order to motivate and inspire.

Developing a leadership portfolio is also a way of modeling best practices. The portfolio has long been recognized as a valuable assessment tool, widely used to assess students' learning, but more recently, as a fairly standard practice for an effective element of faculty development. It is only fitting that the portfolio also become a tool for academic leaders as well, serving as a tool for reflection, documenting personal growth and learning as well as clarifying goals and strategies to achieve them. The portfolio can serve as a document of trust between leaders and followers, providing transparency as well as accountability. It provides leaders an opportunity to articulate the vision while modeling the way.

Concluding Thoughts

We made the point in Chapter 2 that most academic administrators have come from the faculty and, more often than not, were excellent teachers who were recruited into administration because of their innate skills. Job postings for academic administrators usually require teaching and scholarly backgrounds. In this chapter we have tried to show that in the new paradigm, when a faculty member accepts an administrative role, he or she is not leaving behind a set of skills and values. Instead, leaders in the new paradigm will apply their knowledge of good teaching in a new venue, for the best leaders and the best teachers share the same qualities. As we examined the commonalities between good teaching and good leading, we tried to show that the core competencies for both involve human relationships, understanding people, caring about people, and developing the capacity to motivate and inspire them. The best teachers and the best leaders have a deep understanding of the human condition. This understanding of the human factor in fostering learning will be their guide as leaders in the new paradigm.

In short, like the best teachers, the best leaders are competent, forward-thinking individuals who create opportunities for growth and learning through empowering others, with the key defining quality being a keen understanding of people. Whether we are discussing academic administrators, business leaders, or teachers, the fundamental qualities of good leadership remain the same; they are skills related to human behavior and the fundamentals of the human condition. These qualities are consistent with the learner-centered paradigm, for the learner-centered paradigm, unlike the instructional paradigm, values people. It is a humanizing paradigm that fosters human achievement grounded on research from biology, neuroscience, and psychology that provides a scientific framework for understanding human learning.

Earlier we made the claim that adoption of the values of the learner-centered paradigm would bridge the divide that exists between administration and faculty. Understanding the commonality between teaching and leading serves as the first step in that process. In this new paradigm, we share common values, the core value being active learning. By valuing learning, we recognize the conditions that best foster learning—namely community, collaboration, trust, and assessment. In sharing this core value, we place learning at the center of our decision making, regardless of our role within the institution, and regardless of our role within the institution we recognize ourselves as learners working to create an environment conducive to learning for all—students, faculty, and staff.

Chapter Summary

In this chapter we have examined the leadership skills necessary to lead institutions to the new paradigm. We began by exploring the comparison of literature on leadership with literature on the learner-centered paradigm, noting three points of comparison: sharing power, building community, and using assessment for change.

We then present a four-step strategy for change:

1. Recognize the influence of the instructional paradigm on current practices.
2. Realign practices to be consistent with the learner-centered paradigm.
3. Infuse assessment to drive change.
4. Model best practices to make them visible and understandable.

The leadership portfolio is presented as a vehicle for documenting the four-step strategy for change.

Part II

Advancing the
Learner-Centered Agenda

Introduction

In Part I we attempted to make a case for change by presenting the current challenges in higher education that make the time right and by offering perspective on our current paradigm, which is the reason we need to change. A vision for the future, an examination of a new paradigm that can guide the shift and serve as goal state, followed. And finally, we presented the leadership qualities that are needed to make that happen. We quoted Lick (2002), who called for a new breed of leader who is able to lead the new paradigm from rough concept to practical application.

Part II offers examples of practical applications. As we have emphasized previously, these examples are not meant to be prescriptive. They are simply examples of attempts we made when working together as an administrative team to foster change. More important than the results of these experiments is their role as illustrations of the exercise of seeing, revising, experimenting, and adopting new strategies, to make our work intentional rather than guided by habitual blindness.

Content and Structure of Part II

We have chosen four examples of strategies we have implemented. The examples we provide are all related to faculty development. The first focuses on creating community through development opportunities within departments or units. The second is a model for developing interdisciplinary faculty development through a new faculty orientation based on the learning community model. The third is a model for classroom observation that provides a lifelong learning approach to classroom practice. And finally, we illustrate institutional support of faculty development through a capital out-lay project that we redirected toward student learning. In each we will consider the practice in relation to the instructional paradigm and how it could be realigned to the learner-centered paradigm. We will also show how we tried to model the way and incorporate assessment and evaluation, making suggestions in regard to how the leadership portfolio could be used to document the journey to the new paradigm.

5

Fostering Faculty Development

Faculty development is a key element in pushing forward the learner-centered agenda. In discussing leadership in the new paradigm, we made the point that learner-centered leaders believe in development for everyone and they support benchmarks and continuous improvement efforts. In this chapter, we will look at faculty development in relation to communities of practice. As leaders we are asked to consider groups of individuals as well as the institution as a community. We will consider ways in which we can foster faculty development to support the goals of department or unit communities. How will faculty development emerge in the new paradigm? First we will consider the ways in which our current model of faculty development is defined by the instructional paradigm.

Seeing the Influence of the Instructional Paradigm

The model for faculty development in the instructional paradigm is rarely collaborative, nor is it based upon assessment. It tends to be driven by individual agenda or administrative agenda. By *individual agenda,* we refer to the standard model for faculty development that leads toward tenure and promotion. In this model, individual faculty members determine their professional goals, seek funding to support those goals, and then demonstrate the effectiveness of that development through individual accomplishments in teaching, service, and scholarship.

A typical example is the junior faculty member who as a means of attaining tenure sets a goal for the number of papers he or she will present at national conferences and the number of publications, including a mix of manuscripts in refereed journals and book manuscripts. This pattern of development represents the mindset of the instructional paradigm. There is a prescribed number of presentations and publications which must be attained in a prescribed manner. Attaining these goals is highly competitive, and should the individual choose to collaborate on any of them, the individual will lose credit, so to speak, for collaboration does not represent solo achievement. Because of the focus on the number of articles or publications, the goal is not about learning and developing but rather about documenting. Like the student in the instructional paradigm who simply wants to put in the seat time to get the credit for the course in order to get the piece of paper that will assure employment, the focus is not on learning but on credentialing.

The administrative agenda for faculty development is also symptomatic of the instructional paradigm, for it is hierarchical, directed by administration with little choice on the part of the faculty members other than the choice not to attend. A typical example is the administrative goal at an institution to increase the number of courses offered fully online. The decision to move in this direction rarely is based upon student learning but rather is seen as a means for the institution to remain competitive with other institutions vying for student enrollments. Therefore, the administration supports faculty development activities aimed at preparing faculty to teach fully online. Incentives are built in to achieve results. Faculty members are offered cash incentives to develop courses, workload incentives in the form of release time for the first time teaching online and/or lower course caps for online courses, financial support to attend conferences and workshops to gain the necessary expertise to move courses online, and professional recognition in the form of awards for best online teaching. Early adopters gain the most rewards from this type of development opportunity, for more often than not the incentives will dry up as the number of faculty involved increases. The cash incentives become fewer and the workload incentives all but disappear, leaving the faculty feeling animosity toward colleagues who benefited by early adoption and/or feeling tricked by the administration rather than developed. Although this approach might achieve the desired outcome, a learner-centered approach could achieve greater gains.

Realigning with the New Paradigm

In realigning our example of online course development to the new paradigm, the first act would be to move learning to the center of focus rather than enrollment. If we begin looking at enhanced learning as the goal, we set the stage for a completely different discussion for faculty development. In the instructional paradigm model, administrators' goals differed from faculty goals. The administrative goal was to increase enrollment numbers while the faculty goals were focused on pedagogy, increasing the individual's pedagogical repertoire. By placing learning in the central focus, both administration and faculty develop a shared goal, providing an example of the best of shared governance. Shared governance from a learner-centered perspective involves faculty and administrators working together toward a common goal, gaining insight from multiple perspectives.

Both parties begin looking at the online classroom as a new venue for meeting student learning outcomes, thus shifting focus toward determining which courses and curricula are best suited to online delivery. This shift promises a more systematic approach, driven by which learning outcomes can best be achieved by the online format rather than by which faculty member was most willing to experiment with the technology. This is not to say that reduced caps and cash incentives should not be offered. They should. But the development aspect should be contextualized through ongoing discussion and learning about best practices in online teaching relevant to disciplinary goals. This approach fosters a richer and more scholarly approach to the development activities.

Previously we made mention of departmental norms regarding pedagogy. While such norms may be very real, they are rarely discussed or articulated. In fact, some would argue that these norms do not exist because of the autonomy individual faculty have in regard to academic freedom. There is nothing wrong with establishing departmental norms; in fact, we would argue that a healthy and productive discussion of departmental pedagogical norms would be an excellent starting point for faculty development in the new paradigm.

Too often, however, discussions of pedagogy are impressionistic and digress into anecdotal evidence of successes or failures, or worse yet, opportunities to gripe and complain. Brookfield (1995) offers guidelines for fostering critical conversations about teaching, recognizing that these productive conversations require special conditions. Just as classroom teachers know that students need to learn how to function productively in groups, academic leaders must realize that the same is true for faculty. Brookfield (1995) notes that "it is sometimes difficult to get some teachers to see themselves as anything other than independently operating, fully developed and wholly competent professionals. Learning from colleagues might be a concept that is frequently espoused on college campuses, but any attempt to enforce it through mandatory talking circles ensures that any ensuing collegiality is 'contrived'" (p. 140).

Leaders who choose to foster collegial conversations will need to assume the role as teacher and arrange the conditions for learning in order to avoid what Brookfield (1995) characterizes as "teacher talk," talk that is "obsessed with the failings of administrators, the obstructive nature of colleagues in other department, or the annoying loutishness and intellectual limitations of students" (p. 142). Such groups will only work within an organizational framework that is based on trust. He offers questions for establishing ground rules for such groups as well as roles for participants and sample ground rules, demonstrating that careful planning and designing as well as facilitating are a requisite to make this process work.

Because the learner-centered paradigm is evidence-based, driven by assessment and evaluation, we recommend that faculty development in the new paradigm also be driven by assessment and evaluation and that discussions of pedagogy revolve around data and evidence. Faculty development in the learner-centered paradigm should reflect the values of the new paradigm. It should foster collaboration and teamwork while developing community and focus on common core values. Toward achieving that goal, we have experimented with a model for an agenda for faculty development that is based upon assessment and conducted collaboratively, with faculty and administration working in concert toward a common goal.

Assessing Degree of Learner-Centeredness

The course syllabus is an essential component of faculty evaluation because it represents the mindset, the teacher's philosophy of learning, attitude toward students, and conceptualization of the course. When examined collectively, course syllabi can provide a picture of a department or unit's philosophy of learning. An examination of course syllabi for determining the degree of learner-centeredness can provide the department, administrator and faculty, with useable data that can serve as a benchmark as the department or unit works on the goal of shifting teaching practices toward a learner-centered focus (Cullen & Harris, 2009).

We have developed a matrix for assessing learning-centered qualities in course syllabi. This matrix is divided into the three categories we identified in Chapter 3 as characterizing major features of the learner-centered paradigm: (1) community, (2) power and control, and (3) evaluation and assessment. (See Table 5.1, Syllabus Assessment Matrix.)

The first category is community. As we discussed in Chapters 3 and 4, creating a sense of community is a key both in and out

Table 5.1. Syllabus Assessment Matrix

	Highly Instructional (1)	Instructional (2)	Learner-Centered (3)	Highly Learner-Centered (4)
Community				
Accessibility of teacher	Available only for prescribed number of office hours	Available for prescribed number of office hours; provides phone and e-mail	Multiple means of access; encourages interaction	Multiple means of access; requires interaction
Learning rationale	No rationale provided for assignments or activities	Explanation of assignments and activities but not tied directly to learning outcomes	Rationale provided for assignments and activities; tied to learning outcomes	Rationale provided for assignments, activities, methods, policies, and procedures; tied to learning outcomes
Collaboration	Collaboration prohibited	Collaboration discouraged	Collaboration incorporated; use of groups for work and study	Collaboration required; use of groups for class work, team projects
Power and Control				
Teacher role	Rules are written as directives; numerous penalties	Numerous rules with no explanation of relevance; not tied to learning outcomes	Students offered some choice; relevance of rules offered	Students participate in developing policies; rules tied to learning outcomes

Outside resources	No outside resources other than required text	Reference to outside resources provided, but not required	Outside resources encouraged; students responsible for their own learning	Independent investigation required; outside learning required and shared with class
Syllabus focus	Policies and procedures; no discussion of learning or outcomes	Weighted toward policy and procedures with some reference to content covered	Includes course objectives; balance between policies and procedures and focus on learning	Weighted toward learning outcomes and means of assessment; policies are minimal or left to class negotiation

Evaluation and Assessment

Grades	Focus on point deduction; grades used to penalize	Emphasizes accumulation of points disassociated from learning performance	Tied directly to learning outcomes; students have some options for achieving points	Tied to learning outcomes; option for achieving points; not all work is graded
Feedback mechanisms	Mid-term and final test grades only; students not allowed to see or to retain copies of tests	Mid-term and final test grades with minimal other graded work; tests not cumulative; students may see but not retain tests	Grades and other feedback in the form of nongraded assignments, activities, opportunities to conference with teacher	Periodic feedback mechanisms employed for the purpose of monitoring learning

(continued)

Table 5.1. (Continued)

	Highly Instructional (1)	Instructional (2)	Learner-Centered (3)	Highly Learner-Centered (4)
Evaluation	Tests only (not comprehensive)	Tests, quizzes, and other summative evaluation	Multiple means of demonstrating outcomes; some ungraded peer assessment	Multiple means of demonstrating outcomes; self-evaluation and peer evaluation
Learning Outcomes	No outcomes stated	Goals for course stated but not in the form of learning outcomes	Learning outcomes clearly stated	Learning outcomes stated and tied to specific assessments

Source: This matrix is a modified version of the matrix in Roxanne Cullen and Michael Harris, "Assessing learning-centeredness," *Assessment and Evaluation in Higher Education,* 33(1), 2009. doi:10.1080/02602930801956018.

of the classroom. Inside the classroom, fostering community can be achieved through group work and team projects as well as other opportunities to learn from one another, as opposed to the professor being the single source of knowledge. Another facet of community involves relevance. In other words, does the professor attempt to create a sense of relevance to the learning environment by providing rationale for learning and learning activities in order to establish a sense of purpose, trust, and, subsequently, community. The accessibility of the professor is a third indication of community in the sense that it represents investment. The professor who is willing to invest energy and time with students shows a commitment to student learning, which in turn fosters a sense of commitment to learning on the part of the students.

The second matrix category is power and control. As noted previously, intrinsic motivation for learning creates a sense of control over one's learning. Ascertaining students' sense of intrinsic motivation cannot be easily determined by a review of syllabi; however, a syllabus can reveal attempts to create an environment where control is shared. The presentation of policies and procedures and syntax are indicators. The amount of choice provided students is another as well as the responsibilities expected of the student, with the student regarded as partner in the learning experience as opposed to recipient.

The third category is evaluation and assessment. As we have noted earlier, we have made a distinction between evaluation and assessment for both are key to a learning-centered approach. We use *assessment* as ongoing, formative feedback from professor to student to let the student gauge progress as well as feedback from student to professor in order for the professor to determine whether learning is taking place. We use *evaluation* to mean summative determination regarding learning outcomes and whether specific learning outcomes have been met. The more variety in kinds of feedback mechanisms for feedback, including peer assessment and self-assessment, the better.

We have used this matrix to assess the degree of learner-centered practices in departmental units with great success. The process is quite simple. Most institutions collect syllabi as a routine function of administration, keeping them for reference in departmental offices, or in some cases, posting them on websites. So the collection of the data is not an additional duty; it is part of an established routine. We examined a group of syllabi from a small unit of fifteen faculty members. This group of faculty had already committed as a group to a goal of shifting pedagogy toward learner-centeredness and had been working with the Faculty Center on teaching strategies, so they were willing and, in fact, they were eager for our assessment. To illustrate, we reviewed the fifteen syllabi using the matrix and created a table with the results. (See Table 5.2. Sample Assessment of Syllabi.)

Before meeting with the faculty to discuss the results, we made the following observations. The area of greatest strength appears to be in community. The availability of faculty suggests that the teachers are interested and involved in their teaching. The fact that the majority fall in the Instructional (2) column for learning rationale is most likely related to the fact that the numbers are nearly identical to whether learning outcomes are stated on the syllabus. This appeared to us to be a good starting point. It is likely that once the concept of learning outcomes is clearly understood in relation to student learning, the ten teachers who are already providing explanation of assignments and activities will consider tying those explanations to learning outcomes. Evaluation and feedback mechanisms would also appear to be areas for development since there is already fairly good consensus as a group and more movement toward learning-centeredness already apparent in this area. Furthermore, discussion of evaluation and assessment is less threatening than a discussion of power and control, thus making it a favorable starting point for faculty development.

We met with the faculty to discuss our impression of the unit's current state of learner-centeredness based upon the review of

Table 5.2.   Sample Assessment of Fifteen Syllabi

	Highly Instructional (1)	Instructional (2)	Learner-Centered (3)	Highly Learner-Centered (4)
Community				
Accessibility of teacher	7%	40%	53%	—
Learning rationale	7%	66%	27%	—
Collaboration	7%	53%	33%	7%
Power & Control				
Teacher role	33%	60%	7%	—
Outside resources	33%	60%	7%	—
Syllabus focus	33%	53%	14%	—
Evaluation/Assessment				
Grades	27%	66%	7%	—
Feedback mechanisms	—	93%	7%	—
Evaluation	—	66%	33%	—
Learning Outcomes	27%	66%	7%	—

syllabi. We intentionally did not look at individual syllabi nor did we identify syllabi by faculty. We focused the discussion on the similarities among the group and where the group as a whole might focus in terms of continued development. Our discussion was lively and productive. Our role was as designer of a learning experience. We provided the group with data, offered some questions for consideration, and stepped aside while the group formed a plan for their future development, a plan based on data with an objective benchmark.

An examination of this nature provides some real data, something to measure. As we noted earlier, what gets measured gets done. That should be the goal of such a review.

Modeling a Learner-Centered Approach

Modeling the way in regard to faculty development calls upon leaders to demonstrate their commitment to learning and their willingness to acknowledge their need to learn. In our discussion of the similarity between good teachers and good leaders, we made the point that because of these similarities, faculty development for administrators and faculty need not be separate; together administrators and faculty can develop their understanding of learning and teaching/leading. Several benefits can result from this approach. First of all, combining faculty development in this way enhances the notion of a shared vision, thus fostering a sense of community. We all share the same vision and goal, so we can develop together in ways to achieve our ends. Second, it fosters teamwork and collaboration, bringing together various points of view so that everyone gains a fuller understanding from the collaborative process.

We have experimented with this concept of combining faculty and administrative development. We were at a point where a significant number of faculty would be retiring; there was an anticipated turnover of over 50 percent of the faculty in a five-year span. The hiring process, therefore, became an important focal point as it could be used to foster cultural change. Focus on hiring had previously been driven by issues related to policy, especially in regard to affirmative action and other legal concerns. There had been little discussion of strategic hiring in regard to using new positions to reach departmental or college planning objectives. Instead, new positions were usually seen as replacements for the people leaving. Though there was a university goal of achieving diversity, more often than not, hiring committees hired clones of themselves.

We used this as an opportunity for administrators and faculty to develop their focus on hiring in relation to long-term departmental and college goals. This ongoing faculty development initiative was launched with two days of in-service for administrators and faculty with an outside consultant who specialized in the area of visionary hiring. The follow-up to this activity was the selection of a team of administrators and faculty, like the teams we discussed in Chapter 3, charged with developing a program for hiring committees. By working together on this initiative, the act of hiring became an activity with greater meaning and significance than simply finding a replacement faculty member. Because administration and faculty worked together in developing their goals for hiring as well as refining their processes, the result was a process that was less divisive and generally more successful in selecting new candidates.

Development opportunities that include both faculty and administration have the potential to clarify a shared vision, increase awareness of each others' work and challenges, reinforce the need for continuous learning and continuous improvement, and increase transparency. The dichotomy between administration and faculty is reduced by emphasizing the similarities between the two forms of work.

The Leadership Portfolio

The portfolio can be used to examine one's commitment to faculty development. First would be an assessment of the actions taken by leadership to foster faculty development. Second would be a self-assessment focusing on individual learning and growth.

An assessment of one's commitment to faculty development might include an assessment like the one we presented in this chapter which outlines how the need for development was determined as well as the response and support that was provided to meet that need. In the instructional paradigm, it is typical for institutions to assign dollar values to faculty development, simply making the assumption that because so many dollars were spent on development that individuals were developed. The learner-centered paradigm is outcomes based, so rather than focusing on the dollars spent, leadership will want to assess outcomes. What was the outcome of the development activity? Was the money well spent?

In the instructional paradigm, development is documented by vitae, numbers of publications, papers presented, courses taught or developed, conferences attended. In the learner-centered paradigm, it is the outcome that documents the development. A very simple exercise for annually documenting development is to ask, What have I learned this year? Reflection is a key to learning and transformation. Rather than amassing a list of accomplishments, we recommend a reflective essay on one's individual learning which would conclude with goals for the coming year.

In addition to self-assessment, the portfolio should demonstrate that multiple perspectives have been considered. Therefore, faculty perceptions of faculty development opportunities as well as colleague perceptions should be included. Additionally, an examination of the professional literature will round out the reflective assessment.

Chapter Summary

In this chapter, we looked at faculty development in relation to communities of practice. As leaders one of our goals is to establish community. Faculty development offers an opportunity to develop community as we consider how to realign our current practices with the new paradigm.

Four-Step Process

1. In considering how faculty development is governed by the instructional paradigm, we observed that it is driven by either individual goals or administrative goals but that it is rarely collaborative.

2. In considering how to realign faculty development with the learner-centered paradigm, we offered a method for assessing the degree of learner-centeredness within a unit

or department in order to develop unit or department goals as well as to discuss departmental norms in regard to teaching.

3. The method is designed around an assessment practice using the Syllabus Assessment Matrix in order to establish objective and observable criteria that can be used as a benchmark for setting development goals.

4. Leaders can model learner-centered practices by creating opportunities to join faculty and administrative development in order to create a shared vision and to break down the division between faculty and administration.

6

Orienting New Faculty

I n the previous chapter we illustrated a strategy for directing faculty development for units or departments. In this chapter we will expand the vision to an interdisciplinary approach to faculty development. If we are to break down the silos that divide disciplines within the instructional paradigm, we need to foster, encourage, and reward interdisciplinary work. The learning community project is one example of a strategy designed to create cross-disciplinary faculty development.

The New Generation of Faculty

Just as the characteristics of the new generation of undergraduate students, the Millennials, has led educators to reconsider classroom practices, the characteristics of the new generation of academics entering the workforce require reconsideration of institutional policies and procedures. Unlike their predecessors, the new generation of faculty entering the workforce has expressed their increasing dissatisfaction with the traditional academic work environment.

While there have been a number of contributions over the past decade to an evolving view of a new professoriate (Beaudoin, 1998; Anderson, 2002; Baldwin & Chronister, 2002; Boice, 1992; Finkelstein & Schuster, 2001; Moody, 1997), most of the work has focused on the impact of technology on the role of the professoriate and the changing demographics with the increased institutional reliance on part-time positions. Examinations of overall job satisfaction in academe regardless of gender or color have focused on job-related stress (Blackburn & Bentley, 1993; Amey, 1996, Smart, 1990) and collegiality and morale (Copur, 1990; Johnsrud & Rosser, 2002). Hagedorn (2000) and Oshagbemi (1997) offer conceptualizations of job satisfaction. These examinations and others dating back thirty years (Near, Rice, & Hunt, 1978; Nicholson & Miljus, 1972; Hunt & Saul, 1975; DeVries, 1975; Driscoll, 1978) do not address the new generation of scholars now entering the academic workforce.

Many new faculty entering the workforce in 2008 were born as recently as 1980, placing them in the generation popularly known as Generation X, a group characterized as the most stressed and miserable of the various generations from boomers to Millennials (Myron, 2008). Like the Millennials, they have a high affinity for technology and are computer and Internet proficient, but as a generation they are far more skeptical than the Millennials. They tend to change jobs easily in part because they do have challenges unique to their generation, making it difficult for them to achieve the same financial security as their predecessors (Myron, 2008). A *Time* article (Demott, 1987) characterized them as follows:

> By whatever name, so far they are an unsung generation, hardly recognized as a social force or even noticed much at all. . . . By and large [they] scornfully reject the habits and values of the baby boomers, viewing that group as self-centered, fickle and impractical. While the baby boomers had a placid childhood in the 1950s, which helped inspire them to start their revolution, today's twenty-something generation grew up in a time of drugs, divorce and economic strain. . . . They feel influenced and changed by the social problems they see as their inheritance: racial strife, homelessness, AIDS, fractured families and federal deficits.

It is not surprising that this generation of academics entering the workforce would voice their discontent. A recent study of tenure-track faculty sheds light on the generational characteristics of this new cohort of scholars. *The Study of New Scholars* (2002) by Trower and Bleak explored the rising dissatisfaction among new tenure-track faculty. Junior faculty members across the United States were surveyed in order to assess their attitudes and sense of job satisfaction. Such factors as tenure, workload, support for faculty development, climate/collegiality, and policies on such things as performance, research, and service were examined. The three main concerns identified through the survey were (1) the lack of a comprehensible tenure system, (2) lack of community, and (3) lack of an integrated life.

Those surveyed expected to join a collegial, supportive work environment that provided opportunity for a balanced life. They were looking for "communities where collaboration is respected and encouraged, where friendships develop between colleagues within and across departments" (Sorcinelli & Austin, 2000, p. 13). They approached academe with an idealistic, some might claim naïve, conception of the university as a haven for creativity and intellectual camaraderie. Drawn to academic careers because of their love of learning and the perceived opportunity to pursue creative and intellectual interests, they looked forward to being part of a community of scholars. What they discovered was a politicized and, in many respects, antiquated system to which they had to make considerable sacrifice in order to be acculturated.

These findings provide a starting point that can be used to inform institutions as they address the challenges of attracting and keeping new faculty amid an increasing awareness that this new generation of scholars is growing more and more dissatisfied and disillusioned with academic life in the instructional paradigm.

Seeing the Influence of the Instructional Paradigm

The role of the junior faculty member in the instructional paradigm is strikingly similar to that of the student in the instructional paradigm. The junior faculty member finds himself or herself rendered powerless by the tenure process, which in some cases can be secretive with no clear or articulated expectations (Trower and Bleak, 2002). The competitive nature of the process involved in gaining tenure often creates ambiguous and sometimes divisive relationships among junior faculty members and between junior faculty members and their tenured counterparts (Amey, 1996). The process exacerbates the tendency of academe to promote isolation rather than cooperation (Menges & Exum, 1983; Menges, 1999; Seldin, 2006; Gappa, Austin, & Trice, 2007). It pits colleagues against each other in the often ruthless competition for select tenured slots. The rigor of the process does not take into account cultural differences, including such factors as the effect of racial and ethnic background on success (Banks, 1984; Blackburn & Lawrence, 1995; de la Luz Reyes & Halcon, 1988; Menges & Exum, 1983) or the lack of collegiality experienced by people of color (Turner & Myers, 2000). Nor does the system take into account gender differences. Currie, Thiele, and Harris (2002) examined those barriers, both structural, in regard to policies and practices, and cultural, in regard to traditional features of academic culture—all of which have led women to remain in lower ranks with lower pay. Acker (1990), Chliwiniak (1997), and Currie, Thiele, and Harris (2002) also found that women predominate in certain disciplines and in lower ranks within the system. Monroe, Ozyurt, Wrigley, and Alexander (2008) reported on continuing inequality for women including the tendency for women to be steered toward service duties rather than research, subsequently undercutting their chances for tenure and promotion. Other researchers have examined the effect of women's biological clocks in relation to the probationary period and the consequences for advancement of women in academe (Collay, 2002; Cooper & Stevens, 2002; Menges & Exum, 1983). Within this framework, academic administrators often provide "vague, ambiguous, changing, or unrealistic" expectations for new faculty (Sabin, 2007, p. 2), while the tenured faculty members provide conflicting messages regarding achievement of tenure and campus politics. It is no wonder that junior faculty members are disillusioned by this work environment.

Realigning with the New Paradigm

We developed an orientation for newly hired faculty in an effort to respond to the concerns of new scholars as described in the Harvard study and to align our practices with the new paradigm (Harris & Cullen, 2008b). The overarching goal of an orientation program for new faculty is to facilitate their transition into new academic positions by creating a workplace more consistent with a learning organization. In developing our program, we considered the primary goals of the learner-centered organization in relation to the findings of the *Harvard Study of New Scholars*. Based upon our analysis of those findings, we decided that the learning community model would best suit our needs and purpose, for as Gabelnick, MacGregor, Matthews, and Smith (1990) note, learning communities address structural barriers that impede teaching and learning.

Faculty learning communities have proven to be an effective means for tackling institutional challenges (Shapiro & Levine, 1999; Cox & Richlin, 2004). Since the ultimate challenge we are addressing is one of institutional culture, we chose the learning community model as the basis for designing a new faculty orientation program, recognizing that the orientation of new faculty is a single facet in a multifaceted challenge of changing institutional culture.

Learning communities are becoming widely accepted as a means of improving student retention and engagement. The concept of student learning communities dates back to the 1930s (Dewey, 1933; Meiklejohn, 1932), when the idea of cohorts of students taking similar courses was initiated. The movement finally became solidified through the work at Evergreen State University in the 1980s (Jones, 1981). Similarly, faculty learning communities have become a standard feature of faculty development offerings. Cox (2004) defines a faculty learning community as a group of six to fifteen cross-disciplinary faculty "who engage in active, collaborative, yearlong programs with a curriculum about enhancing teaching and learning and with frequent seminars and activities that provide learning development, the scholarship of teaching and community building" (p. 8). Cox (2004) identifies ten qualities that must be present to foster community:

1. *Safety and trust.* Participants must feel safe to reveal weaknesses or ignorance of teaching processes or literature.

2. *Openness.* Participants must feel safe to share thoughts and feelings without fear of retribution.

3. *Respect.* The university must acknowledge their participation through financial support.

4. *Responsiveness.* Participants must respond respectfully to one another.

5. *Collaboration.* Groups must have the ability to respond to one another. Joint projects and presentations should also be welcomed.

6. *Relevance.* Learning outcomes are enhanced by relating subject matter to participants' teaching, courses, and scholarship.

7. *Challenge.* Expectations should be high.

8. *Enjoyment.* Social opportunities should be included.

9. *Esprit de corps.* Sharing individual and group outcomes should generate a sense of pride.

10. *Empowerment.* Empowerment is a desired learning outcome. Participants should gain new insight to themselves and new sense of confidence in their abilities. (p. 19)

These requirements of the learning community reflect the learner-centered agenda particularly in regard to the building of community. Inside the classroom, learner-centered teachers work to establish an environment of safety and trust, a space where experimentation and error are expected rather than chastised. They employ collaborative strategies in order to empower learners and create relevance to the learning. Standards are kept high, and learning outcomes are made explicit. As we discussed in Chapter 4, learner-centered leaders have the same goals in regard to establishing community. These ten qualities of the learning community are ten qualities we strive for in building a learner-centered campus.

In an attempt to show respect for their time and cooperation, the new faculty in our orientation community were paid a stipend to meet for a week-long program prior to the beginning of classes, prior to the return of the other faculty. The objective of meeting at this time was to create an opportunity for the new faculty to bond with one another prior to being introduced to their department or unit colleagues. Typically within the instructional paradigm framework, faculty orientations, if conducted at all, take place within departments. College tenure policies typically recommend that new faculty begin service work within their department, then their college, and finally at the university level. This often results in new faculty going several years without meeting colleagues outside their own department or college.

We had our Faculty Center conduct the majority of the programming. Because of the importance of the Faculty Center to teaching, learning, and scholarship, we wanted to establish a rapport between staff at the Center and the new faculty to facilitate their transition to the institution and to begin what we hope to be a long-term relationship based on scholarship and teaching. The Center in its role as a safe haven for faculty is key to establishing culture of honest inquiry, providing confidential, formative support and advice as well as a variety of services to support faculty teaching and scholarship outside the context of departmental review or administrative oversight.

Though we had the orientation programming conducted primarily by Center staff, the administrative team of deans and department heads also played a role akin to learner-centered teacher, establishing themselves as mentors and facilitators of the new faculty's future success. First, the deans and department heads attended the planned programming to emphasize the concept that everyone is a learner in a learner-centered organization. Further, we encouraged the deans and department heads to spend time learning about the new members of their colleges. At the college and department level, we resisted providing prepackaged orientation materials, a one-size-fits-all approach. Instead, we asked the deans and department heads to sit down with each new faculty member, get to know him or her, and talk about the individual's expectations of the new position. Likewise, this was an opportunity to give clear goals in terms of the institution's expectations of the new faculty member. By individualizing the discussion of goals and expectations, we were able to establish a sense of shared power. Goals were not mandated, but instead discussed and even sometimes negotiated. By shifting responsibility to the deans and department heads, we also sought to decentralize the authority and responsibility for the program by shifting power to the colleges.

As leadership of the division, we also met with the new faculty and took part in the sessions. Reiterating the point to the new scholars in the presence of their deans and department heads that as an organization, we encouraged experimentation while recognizing that some experiments fail, emphasizing the literature on failure as a stepping stone to success and a key to establishing a mindset for continuous improvement. We also emphasized that as an organization, we recognized that students are often resistant to the learner-centered pedagogical techniques. The implementation of those strategies could very likely lead to unfavorable student evaluations but the department heads and deans would recognize this and be supportive of the new faculty's continued efforts to implement new strategies with ongoing assessment and reflection.

We also incorporated a number of social activities in order to foster a sense of community. We believe that it is important to hold activities for entire families in order to foster a sense of belonging. These activities also send the message that we do understand the balance needed between work and family and that as an institution, we value family and respect the need for a balanced life. These events included tenured faculty and administrators as well as selected individuals from the local community. The social activities were held off campus in casual settings to promote both a sense of ease and friendship among the group and to flatten or balance the perceived hierarchy or power relationships between tenured faculty, administration, and the new faculty.

After the first week of intense programming, the community met weekly with staff from the Faculty Center for the remainder of the academic year. We also met with them periodically throughout the year. They studied together, planned their courses together, and discussed scholarship and opportunities for service. The community met weekly for the entire first year, discussing topics related to teaching, scholarship, and engagement. In order to foster the spirit of collaboration and interdisciplinarity, we provided support for faculty development activities for the group.

In the spirit of transferring responsibility for learning to the learners, we asked the new faculty learning community to take a major role in planning the orientation for the next year's learning community. They did so with tremendous enthusiasm.

Assessing the Process

Based on our experiences implementing this program at more than one university and using feedback from participants in order to continually improve upon it, we recommend building various assessment opportunities into the programming. First, to determine the effectiveness of the initial first week program, a survey of the new faculty at the close of the week-long program can provide feedback about individual sessions and workshops and ask for suggestions for next year's programming.

We also recommend conducting surveys midway through the first semester and midway through the second semester in order both to gain feedback on the effectiveness of the programming and to determine if attitudinal changes occur during the first year of service. We developed a simple survey loosely modeled on the College Student Expectations Questionnaire (CSXQ) and the College Student Environment Questionnaire (CSEQ), two instruments developed by George Kuh of Indiana University to compare student expectations of college with their subsequent experiences. Like the CSXQ, our initial survey elicits questions about expectations regarding teaching, scholarship, service, collegiality, and expected time commitment to various activities. The subsequent survey focuses on campus environment relative to teaching, scholarship, service, and collegiality in relation to what they experienced.

In order to gain additional feedback, it is useful for deans and department heads to meet with new faculty individually and to meet the new faculty within their college as a group at least twice during the semester. This not only provides feedback but also enables the deans and department heads to continue their role as mentors, fostering community.

To gain further insight to the goal of creating community, we suggest interviewing the group two and three years later to find whether they continue to collaborate with colleagues from their learning community. When we have done this, we have limited these interviews to two specific questions asked of each participant along with open-ended questions to elicit general feedback. First, "Do you collaborate with the members of your learning community within your college?" and second, "Do you collaborate with the members of your learning community outside your college?"

Our main goal was to establish a sense of community among the group, and we have had great success with this model at more than one institution. In general, the surveys and interviews indicated that the majority maintained contact with other group members outside their own discipline. A majority of comments pointed to the fact that they appreciated having contact with faculty outside their discipline, particularly in regard to discussing concerns about tenure and political issues within their departments.

Modeling a Learner-Centered Approach

It could be argued that nowhere is it more important to model the way than in our interactions with new faculty. If we believe that our hiring practices are tied to our vision for the future, then our care and tending of new faculty are essential in bringing about that vision. Over and over, literature on leadership admonishes leaders to walk their talk, to put their vision into action. New faculty are in a unique position of becoming acculturated to a new environment. Their perceptions are important, for they can provide useful feedback on the connection between a community's perception of itself and the reality since they are coming into the community as outsiders. People in these situations are learning the beliefs and behaviors of the culture they are joining, and they can offer fresh and untainted perspectives. Too often new faculty orientation reflects the values of the instructional paradigm, asking the new faculty member to change in order to fit the existing culture. If we truly believe in diversity and community, then we will not expect the new faculty to conform; rather, we will explore what they have to bring to our culture to enhance, deepen, and expand our character and opportunities. Everyone will be in the position of learner, not only the new faculty.

Leaders leading the shift to the learner-centered paradigm are in a unique position because the entire community is, essentially, going through a process of acculturation, not only the new faculty. It is a time, then, for community discussion and examination of values, beliefs, and customs. Therefore, it is incumbent upon leaders to foster a sense of trust and openness for such discussion and to take part in it. As we discussed earlier, part of establishing trust involves seeing mistakes as part of the learning process and admitting our own mistakes and the need to improve.

Experienced teachers know that one of the most basic tenets of teaching is never to pretend to know something that they don't and to admit mistakes quickly, rectify, and move on. Students have far greater confidence in teachers who themselves have the confidence to admit a mistake. Those who refuse to admit error cannot gain the trust of or inspire confidence in others. They simply look foolish and stubborn. We understand this as teachers, but somehow it becomes much harder to practice outside the classroom as faculty colleagues and academic leaders.

While unfortunately we have witnessed this on various occasions, one example stands out because of its absurdity and dramatic consequence. We watched a dean completely self-destruct and lose all confidence of her faculty because of her unwillingness to admit that she made a bad call in regard to a policy on travel reimbursement. In spite of the longstanding policy that meals were reimbursed on a per diem basis, she insisted on collecting receipts to assure that the amount of the meal was less than or equal to the per diem. When the faculty and the faculty association challenged her, she refused to accept that she was wrong. In order to capture an insignificant amount of funding, she dug in her heels and refused to admit that her judgment had been poor.

This incident had a domino effect on other pending issues in the college. An atmosphere of distrust developed and ultimately resulted in a vote of no confidence in the dean and her subsequent resignation. How different this situation might have been had she had the confidence to admit that her decision was poor, rectify it, and move on. How different the climate in the college would have been had the faculty believed that she trusted them, both in regard to her original decision about the policy as well as her willingness to admit a mistake.

In creating a sense of community, it is also essential to reinforce the idea that all members contribute and bring distinct knowledge, attitudes, and points of view that enrich the community. The acculturation of new faculty in the instructional paradigm was predominantly a one-way process requiring the new member to adjust and fit into the existing community. The new paradigm recognizes the value of each member and is more pluralistic in design, suggesting that the concept of adjusting to a dominant community be replaced by the concept of an evolving diverse community that continuously changes and improves because of the interaction of the changing identities within the group.

The Leadership Portfolio

The leader's portfolio should document the work done with new hires. Leaders will want to consider the success of their part in the new faculty members' transition to the institution. In reflecting on the process, feedback from faculty and colleagues will inform one's self-assessment. Because leaders at different levels of the hierarchy have different interactions with new faculty as well as different vantage points, colleague consultation and exchange is an important aspect of this reflection. While the orientation program itself might be an outstanding success, the process of assisting individuals to find their professional selves and develop authenticity in their roles takes time and will be informed by the various perspectives of colleagues from different colleges and different levels of the organization. We will want to assess progress of individuals as well as have the opportunity to consider cohorts of new hires in order to gather a view of larger institutional goals and whether we are making progress toward them.

Chapter Summary

This chapter described a new faculty orientation program based on the learning community model. The interdisciplinary approach was intended to encourage new faculty to work with colleagues outside of their disciplines and to develop a sense of community.

The rising dissatisfaction with academic jobs among Generation X faculty can be attributed to the influence of the instructional paradigm. By realigning the process of orienting new faculty to be consistent with the new paradigm, we hope that new faculty will find their work more satisfying as they develop a sense of community with colleagues across the campus.

Four-Step Process

1. In considering how faculty orientation is governed by the instructional paradigm, we observed that it is often a case of the individual being acculturated to departmental norms, placing the junior faculty in a vulnerable position to tenured colleagues and administration.

2. In considering how to align faculty orientation with the learner-centered paradigm, we offered a learning community model focused on mentoring and cross-disciplinary support.

3. Assessment is part of the ongoing process, both assessing the response of participants to the process and also assessing long-term to see if the process has the intended effect.

4. Leaders can model learner-centered practices by creating an environment of trust and an atmosphere where experimentation is promoted and mistakes are part of the learning.

7

Assessing Teaching Quality

I n Chapter 3 we told the story of a colleague who employed collaborative teams in her classroom only to be judged as having lost
control of her students by colleagues who did not understand the
concept. This professor was fortunate to have a department head
that understood the pedagogy and was supportive of her. We also
used the example of the new faculty member who came under attack
by her tenure committee for employing pedagogical strategies that
deviated from the norm of her department. In each case, the academic administrator became pivotal in resolving the disputes. What
a difference if the administrator would have led the change instead
of just reacting to leadership by faculty.

On a very practical level, academic administrators need to
understand, embrace, and advocate learner-centered teaching if it is
to move beyond the periphery of the institution and become mainstream pedagogy. Also because academic administrators will have
the job of evaluating learner-centered teachers and must deal with
student and sometimes faculty resistance to the pedagogy, they must
be well versed in the learner-centered approach.

This chapter focuses on the role of the academic administrator in faculty evaluation, with a specific focus on assessing quality
teaching. We envision the assessment of teaching quality as a more
formative process in the learner-centered paradigm, one that is not
conducted solely for monitoring new hires but instead is a community building opportunity fostering continuous improvement and
lifelong learning for all teaching faculty, setting the expectation

for faculty to continuously improve and add to their repertoire of teaching strategies throughout their careers.

Seeing the Influence of the Instructional Paradigm

Teaching evaluation in the instructional paradigm is most often a summative affair conducted by administration and peers for the purpose of determining an individual's continued employment and acceptability for tenure. The view of teaching in the instructional paradigm has been largely performance based with the focus on the transmission of knowledge. After all, the synonym for the word *professor* is *lecturer*, one who imparts knowledge. Underlying this belief is the assumption that if students don't learn, it is their fault. Tradition within this paradigm presupposes that if the professor knows the discipline, then that is sufficient. While graduate education is making strides to rectify this situation, it is still common for professors to be provided little or no instruction in the role that represents a major element of their responsibility: teaching. Even in institutions that identify themselves as teaching institutions, where the focus is on undergraduate education, teaching is not always evaluated with an eye for continuous improvement, but rather for maintaining basic standards of quality. In some disciplines it is typical for new assistant professors to have had no classroom teaching experience, and if they are ineffective, it is usually not discovered until after complaints or crisis. Likewise, tenure, promotion, and merit have historically been tied to activities other than teaching, as some believe that teaching is not as valuable as research and that good teaching can't be measured or that little can be done if someone is a bad teacher. The lack of emphasis on teaching in the consideration of promotion and merit reduces the incentive for tenured faculty to expend energy on continuous improvement of their teaching effectiveness, for there is little reward in doing so.

The metrics of faculty evaluation have been a source of discussion and contention for decades. Seldin (1993) conducted surveys in the 1970s and early 1980s to identify how faculty evaluation was being conducted. He found that quality of teaching was determined primarily by student ratings, course syllabi, and examinations. Seldin (2006) outlined a list of barriers to successful evaluation, the first of which was social and attitudinal problems associated with traditional academic biases. Centra's surveys (1993) revealed similar findings. These barriers to successful evaluation are consistent with the values of the instructional paradigm. These practices are consistent with the values of the instructional paradigm. The hierarchical nature of the paradigm prioritizes the department chair's and dean's evaluation and treats grades on examinations as validation that knowledge has been successfully transferred from professor to student. Evaluation of teaching is made as objective as possible through use of exam scores and student ratings, with the evaluation focused on the performance of the professor demonstrating technical expertise in delivery of knowledge.

A recent case of a faculty member's dismissal illustrates the challenge faced by students, faculty, and administration regarding student learning within the context of the instructional paradigm. A biology professor at a major university that serves a high proportion of minority students from disadvantaged backgrounds was dismissed because he repeatedly assigned grades of D and F to the majority of his students. He maintained that he was simply holding to standards. The university claimed that he was "unwilling to compromise" and pass more students. Reportedly the dean had set the expectation that 70 percent of the students should pass. The faculty member described his job as "imparting knowledge onto" students. (Jaschik, 2009, p. 1). The discussion of this very complicated and difficult issue that many universities are facing is couched in the language of the instructional paradigm. The focus is on grades and an arbitrary percentage set for passing. Everyone blamed someone: the administration blamed the faculty; the faculty blamed the students as well as the administration. This cycle of blame is a characteristic of the instructional paradigm, where, as Tagg (2003) writes,

"It is the nature of the organizational defensive routines to allow free exercise of blame and self-righteousness while insulating the system from fundamental improvement" (p. 21). Nowhere in the discussion was there mention of student learning. This unfortunate story is an example of the instructional paradigm at work.

Tradition and acceptable practice have dictated that knowledge of a specific discipline is sufficient for the transmission of that knowledge to students; however, we know that it is not enough just to know one's discipline. Teaching one's discipline is very different from "imparting" one's discipline. While great teachers throughout history have understood this difference and while the study of effective teaching and learning is certainly not new, the discussion of teaching and learning on college campuses has been all but mute until recently.

Our new understanding of what constitutes effective learning has prompted a discussion of pedagogy on campuses—two-year, four-year, public and private, nationwide—unlike any time previously. Huber and Hutchings (2005) write in *The Advancement of Learning*: "For most of the history of higher education in the United States, the form and content of the curriculum have been the most common sites for realigning college studies with changes in the larger social and scholarly worlds. What makes today's situation unusual is that pedagogy has finally slipped off the cloak of tradition and like other institutions of cultural transmission that are no longer taken for granted, become 'controversial, conscious, constructed: a matter of decision, will and effort'" (p. 7). While the discussion of pedagogy has become acceptable on college campuses, there is still much work to be done in revising our long-standing practices of assessing teaching quality.

Realigning with the New Paradigm

In the instructional paradigm, the professor's delivery of knowledge is the central focus in reviews of teaching quality. Fairly established criteria are used by reviewers when determining the quality of performance, including such characteristics as organization of content, use of visual aids, eye contact, and clarity of expression. However, in the learner-centered paradigm the professor's role is one of designer, so the standard measures require realignment with the new paradigm. Rather than focusing on the delivery of content, the reviewer is looking at the design of learning opportunities, the repertoire of the designer in relation to the content discipline, and the success of those choices in relation to student learning. We recognize, of course, that there is no reliable way to tie teaching methods to learning gains because there are so many variables to consider; however, in judging the quality of teaching, one can determine whether teachers are attempting to monitor the effectiveness of their pedagogical choices and assessing student learning continuously throughout each course. In realigning with the new paradigm, which prioritizes continuous improvement in a community where it is safe to experiment and take risks, we will need to shift from summative evaluation to formative assessment (Harris & Cullen, 2008a).

Assessment of quality of teaching then is conducted with an eye for intentionality on the part of the teacher, with an awareness that his or her expertise in the discipline relates to instructional design and subsequently the orchestration of that design in the learning environment. The underlying expectation of teaching quality is that as faculty members become more expert in their disciplines and in their teaching, they will establish a wider repertoire of pedagogical choices and continue to refine their teaching strategies.

Assessing teaching quality in the learner-centered paradigm must be realigned with the goals, purposes, and values of the paradigm, including such features as a recognition and tolerance for individual differences and creation of community through fostering collaboration and teamwork, an assumption of lifelong learning and continuous improvement, a balance of power and control, and a reliance on outcomes and assessment. Ultimately the process depends on how well the reviewer understands human learning and the learner-centered paradigm. As Bain (2004) writes, "It requires faculties to talk about the nature of learning in the field and begin to craft an epistemological literature in each discipline and course. It demands attention to the science of human learning, to the vast and growing body of research and theoretical literature on how people learn, what it means to learn, and how best to foster it" (p. 170).

In *Assessing Faculty Work* (1994), Braskamp and Ory discuss faculty assessment in terms of the Latin root of *assess*, "to sit beside" (p. 15). They use this as a metaphor for formative assessment of faculty work. This metaphor provides a helpful starting point for thinking about assessing learner-centered teaching, for it requires collegial and thoughtful discussion and examination of the process and the outcomes. It also requires academic administrators to be well versed in the learner-centered paradigm. If in leading the new paradigm, we are to "sit beside" the faculty member and have a thoughtful discussion of the faculty member's teaching, we must have enough background to know the questions to ask as well as the advice to offer.

Best practices in assessment call for multiple measures, and the assessment of teaching quality is no different. Arreola (2007) developed a multidimensional model that serves as an excellent example. Faculty jointly work to identify the dimensions of their role and then identify measures for assessment. Such measures should minimally include classroom observation, discussion with the faculty member, a teaching portfolio that documents the courses taught, peer review, and student ratings. Chickering's (2000) definition of teaching as "arranging conditions for learning" can serve as the basis of truly meaningful, relevant, and constructive evaluation of teaching. What has the professor done to arrange conditions for learning? What choices have been made and for what intent or purpose? The resulting questions then become, Were the choices effective? and How does the professor know? Hatfield (1995) provides a series of inventories based on Chickering and Gamson's article "Seven Principles of Good Practice in Undergraduate Education" (1987) which can be very helpful for developing faculty in this area. The inventory asks the faculty member ten questions related to the seven principles: encouraging student-faculty contact, encouraging cooperation among students, encouraging active learning, providing prompt feedback, emphasizing time on task, communicating high expectations, and respecting diverse talents and learning styles (Hatfield, 1995, pp. 117–124). Inventories like these provide the faculty member a means of establishing clear and specific goals in each of the seven principles of good practice and showing how he or she is arranging conditions for learning.

As reviewers, we will want to guide faculty members in this developmental process, helping them to reflect upon the effectiveness of their choices in design and application. In doing so, we will need to be sensitive to issues of power and control, to attitudes toward learning—both student and teacher—and to the many forms of assessment and evaluation and their use in various contexts. We must also be comfortable with the language for writing learning objectives and learning outcomes and be familiar with techniques for active lecturing, problem-based learning, concept mapping, effective discussion techniques, and more.

Classroom Observation

Of the many techniques for assessing teaching quality that are part of the academic administrator's responsibility, classroom observation provides numerous challenges in the new paradigm. How does one begin to ascertain the professor's control of the class, for example, when a goal is for the professor to relinquish control? If students are encouraged to take responsibility for their own learning, how does one assess the professor's role in that process?

Let us consider how we might approach classroom observation in the new paradigm. Our assessment process should reflect the very elements we are trying to promote in the classrooms of those we are assessing. In short, our assessment of teaching effectiveness should model best teaching practices. To do that, first we must model a belief that intelligence is expandable. That translates to a belief that teaching is something that can be learned and improved upon. Second, we want to contextualize the learning. What knowledge, experience, and motivation to learn does the individual bring to his or her teaching? And finally, how can our process create opportunities that empower individuals and encourage experimentation and risk taking? The learner-centered paradigm calls for viewing issues from multiple perspectives and taking into account that learning is not confined to fifty-minute increments. From this vantage point, the actual classroom visit plays a minor role compared to the assessment of teaching effectiveness overall. The classroom observation will become an opportunity to assess the orchestration of teaching goals and, as such, serve as one source of data in this assessment process.

At least three data sources can be used to examine teaching philosophy and pedagogical stance: a teaching philosophy statement, the course syllabus, and discussion about teaching. In Chapter 5 we introduced the idea of using course syllabi for assessment data, examining groups of syllabi to determine degree of learner-centeredness in a department or unit in order to guide professional development. The matrix we developed for this purpose (Table 5.1) examines fairly gross features. In this chapter, we will look more closely at the course syllabus as a document that reveals individual teaching strategies and approaches to learning.

The Syllabus

We have found that reading the course syllabus prior to reading the teaching philosophy or having a discussion with the reviewee is a productive strategy. As we stated in Chapter 5, a syllabus is more than a course outline. It represents the teacher's mindset, philosophy of learning, attitude toward students, and conceptualization of the course. It is also most often the first document presented to students and serves as an introduction to the course and the professor. For those reasons we place considerable emphasis on the syllabus, reading it both from the perspective of the student and the administrator, asking these questions: What is the initial impression the document will make upon the student? and Does the document reflect knowledge of the learner-centered paradigm?

In an article in *Change Magazine*, Mano Singham (2005) provided a thoughtful examination of the effect of the syllabus on student learning, noting that over time the syllabus has become a legal protection, or as he calls it, "a defensive shield" for faculty, so its language reflects what he calls a "creeping authoritarianism." Likewise, syllabi have grown in length as faculty, sometimes at the direction of administrators, try to anticipate every possible student maneuver. He writes, "By devising complex general rules to cope with any and all anticipated behavior, we tend to constrain, alienate, and dehumanize students and we remove a great deal of the enjoyment from the learning experience" (p. 57). Much of the authoritarian language of syllabi has become deeply entrenched in our educational systems, and teaching faculty have learned to view the syllabus as a protective safeguard. This mindset betrays an adversarial relationship between faculty and students, of which many faculty members are not consciously aware. Administrators can work closely with faculty, helping them to carefully select language which fulfills legal necessities without coming across as hostile, aggressive and authoritarian. We will provide some examples later in this section.

As we illustrated in Chapter 5, a syllabus for a course that is striving to be learner-centered should include some of the key elements that define the learner-centered approach, namely, an attempt to create community, a sharing of power and control over what is learned and how it is learned, as well as assessment and evaluation tied directly to learning outcomes. The clear articulation of learning outcomes and clear methods of assessing those outcomes is a fundamental requirement of learner-centered pedagogy.

A sense of community can be assessed in several ways. For one, accessibility of the teacher signals interest in the students' learning and willingness to participate in this community of learners. It is also the first of the seven principles of good practice. Accessibility of the teacher can be determined by the number of office hours and multiple means of contact (phone, home phone, e-mail, etc.). Harder to assess objectively yet equally important is the overall language of the document in regard to the attitude toward students and teaching. However, one does not need to be a rhetorician to recognize the difference in tone and effect among the following excerpts from syllabi:

1. You will attend class regularly.
2. Each semester I fail students for not attending class. Don't be one of them.
3. Attendance is mandatory.
4. Effort and engagement are two of several factors that are part of the "discretionary" percentage of your final grade. Therefore I will take attendance daily to monitor your effort and engagement.
5. Attending class regularly is the best way to succeed in this class. Research has shown that the single most important factor in student success is attendance. Simply put, going to class greatly increases your ability to succeed. In order to support your ability to succeed, I have made attendance a factor in your final grade. This should be the easiest outcome for you to achieve in this class.

Is the language encouraging, inclusive, a first attempt at rapport in establishing a community of learners, or does the language establish lines of authority and control? The excerpts above provide a range in authoritarian stance: 1 and 2 illustrate teacher dominance; 1 is an imperative, demanding attendance, and 2 is hostile in the form of a sarcastic threat. Excerpt 3 opts for the passive voice to avoid an outright demand but maintains the power of the professor. Excerpts 4 and 5 are friendlier in tone, trying to provide a rationale as well as relevance for the attendance requirement.

Teachers sharing information about themselves, revealing their background and experience or professional interests, also shows an attempt at creating community. Sharing information in this way gets back to our emphasis on the human element involved in good teaching and leading, and it creates a human interest, going a long way toward establishing credibility and authenticity.

Shared power is another major feature of the learner-centered paradigm. Recall in Chapter 3 the teacher who experimented with sharing power by allowing students to determine policies for attendance and late work. Maryellen Weimer (2002) describes a menu approach to assignments that she designed, giving students various options for demonstrating their achievement of learning outcomes. These examples may represent the far end of the spectrum of power sharing. Numerous subtler ways that teachers share power can usually be found on the syllabus. Are students given any opportunity for choice? Are there options for meeting requirements? Is any leniency built into the explanation of policies, or are the policies stated as absolutes? Any opportunities for students to choose—whether it is self-selection of groups for group work or optional reading assignments—are examples of teachers sharing power, and students recognize them as such.

Evaluation and assessment are also key indicators of learner-centeredness. Are the learning outcomes clearly stated and tied to assessment and evaluation measures? Does the teacher employ both formative assessments and summative evaluations? Is assessment and evaluation ongoing throughout the semester, or is there only a mid-term and a final? Are the assessments used as learning tools, or do students simply get grades posted? How do students know what their grades are, and how is grading presented on the syllabus? All these factors give insight to the approach to teaching as well as attitudes and beliefs about students and learning.

Statement of Philosophy

A statement of philosophy should be part of the assessment measures, as it is a document that can help the administrator prepare for the preobservation visit. Several resources on the development of a learner-centered syllabus recommend incorporating such a statement (Weimer, 2002; Grunert, 1997; O'Brien, Millis, & Cohen, 2008; Beaudry & Schaub, 1998). New faculty, in particular, should be provided with guidelines for developing a statement of philosophy. There are numerous sources available on the development of a statement of teaching philosophy; perhaps the most often cited is Nancy Van Note Chism's (1998) essay prepared for the Professional Organizational Development (POD) network. In this essay she offers five key components to be considered in the development of such a statement: (1) conceptualization of learning, (2) conceptualization of teaching, (3) goals for students, (4) implementation of philosophy, and (5) professional growth plan.

Because of the importance of intentionality in the assessment of teaching quality, as we have emphasized, the philosophy statement is an important document, providing a written statement of one's intentions. Many of the guidelines available to writers of teaching statements recommend the use of metaphors to articulate one's conception of teaching. Grasha's (1996) compendium of metaphors for learning provide choices for writers of teaching statements, including the teacher as tour bus driver, midwife, gardener, rabbi, or master. Individuals' choices of metaphors can provide insight to their conception of teaching. Of equal interest is whether the claims in the teaching philosophy statement are borne out in the syllabi, discussions, and observation. Is the implementation of the philosophy consistent? In other words, is the philosophy practiced as well as espoused?

We have emphasized that the assessment of teaching quality in the learner-centered paradigm should focus on the choices that teachers make. The philosophy statement should attempt to explain the rationale for choosing particular strategies. Later in this chapter when we talk about peer review, we will discuss critical characteristics of one's courses. For each course, the teacher should identify critical characteristics that define that course, features that differentiate it from other courses. For example, if a person is teaching a course that serves as an introduction to a discipline, the first course in a major that students are required to take as a prerequisite for other major courses, then the critical characteristics of the course might read as follows: (1) this course introduces students who have elected this major to the discipline; (2) this course prepares students to take courses X, Y, and Z; (3) students in this course are usually first-semester freshmen; (4) students are usually motivated to take this course because it is the only course in their major that they take as freshmen. These critical characteristics become a backdrop for the pedagogical choices that the teacher makes. The characteristics help the teacher, before actually meeting the students, to identify background, readiness, and motivation of students as well as content and skill development needed as a prerequisite for courses X,Y, and Z. The reviewer then also has a richer context to assess the teaching strategies employed, and if there are issues or problems, they can be discussed as a misjudgment of what constituted the critical characteristics, providing the reviewer with a neutral, less threatening way to discuss shortcomings.

Chism (1998) also suggests that the philosophy statement include professional goals, a growth plan. Discussion of the growth plan provides a nice opportunity for the administrative reviewer not only to guide faculty development but also to indicate up front how much support will be available to help individuals achieve their goals.

Discussion with Faculty

A preobservation discussion serves as the opportunity to "sit beside," to establish a rapport between the observer and the observed. Millis (2006) describes a three-step process to classroom observation. The discussion can cover both the larger issues of teaching philosophy as well as the craft of teaching and, if possible, understanding of the discipline. (We recognize that some academic administrators are responsible for faculty evaluation outside their specific academic discipline, which will necessarily limit the discussion of academic discipline.)

Prior to observing a class, the reviewer wants to know how the lesson being observed fits into the larger scheme of the course, in terms of both content and pedagogy and what the teacher is trying to accomplish. What are the learning goals for this specific class, and what are the techniques employed to achieve the goal? What will students have been asked to do prior to class to prepare, and how will the work of that day be carried through in subsequent class sessions?

One of the key attributes of the learner-centered pedagogy is understanding who the students are, what knowledge and attitudes they bring to the course. With this knowledge, the teacher can adapt and link current learning to previous learning in order to achieve the best results. In order to begin to assess this, the administrator can ask questions to determine how well the teacher knows the students. Are students referred to by name? In what way does the teacher offer examples of the learning or background of individual students? Did the teacher conduct any sort of precourse survey to find out information about the students? Did the teacher conduct any sort of initial diagnostic to determine students' level of learning? All these are indicators of that more nebulous characteristic described by Bain (2004) as creating community and trusting in students.

The preobservation discussion can be a rich source of information regarding teaching philosophy, competence in the discipline, and knowledge of teaching craft. The actual observation, then, becomes an opportunity to compare the findings of the preobservation discussion. The observation obviously will vary according to the preobservation discussion. Ideally, the observer wants to walk into the classroom knowing the learning outcomes expected for that class period and the techniques that will be employed. The observation is also an opportunity to assess the sense of community that has been established.

The postobservation visit is, again, an opportunity to "sit beside," to discuss what the teacher thought of the class, what worked well, what might be changed in the future, what didn't work, and so forth. The postobservation discussion is the most demanding for the administrator because this is when true, in-depth discussion of pedagogical strategies will take place. Deep knowledge of learner-centered teaching strategies and learning theory is required. One way of approaching the postobservation discussion would be to ask the teacher if he or she believes that the learning outcomes for that day were met and how that was determination made. What method of assessment was used to measure the learning for that class? This discussion can lead into a more in-depth discussion of the difference between assessment and evaluation. Does the teacher use ongoing assessment to assure that learning is taking place? How does the teacher adjust in relation to that ongoing feedback? If multiple observations are possible, the postobservation visit is the time to plan on a subsequent visits. Subsequent visits offer the opportunity to see how the rapport of the class changes as the semester proceeds and how the teacher has adjusted to ongoing assessment of student learning.

Student Ratings

Student ratings have been the subject of a considerable body of research in higher education. Well over one thousand articles have been published presenting research evidence. Wilbert McKeachie (1996), perhaps best known for his widely used book of teaching tips, claims that "we probably have more good research on student ratings than on any other aspect of higher education" (p. 4). Still, controversy over their reliability and use continues. Herman Remmers, whose four decades of research on student ratings are widely considered the best on the subject, found that student ratings are quite reliable and generally correlated to student learning. Williams and Ory (1992) found that class size had negligible effect on ratings, though small classes have a slight advantage. Discipline can also be a factor. Cashin (1990) studied ratings from over 100,000 classes and found that ratings tend to be higher in arts and humanities, followed by biological and social sciences, with math, engineering, and physical sciences at the bottom. Most interesting, however, is that difficulty level of the class did not play a role in ratings.

Contrary to popular belief, working harder correlated with higher ratings from students, not the reverse. Murray, Rushton, and Paunonen (1990) found that students rate professors highly who are knowledgeable, approachable, and enthusiastic about their discipline and about their teaching. Though widely believed, the notion that easy teachers get higher ratings has not been proven to be true. As Braskamp and Ory (1994) aptly noted, "Neither the 'stand up comic' with no content expertise nor the 'cold-fish expert' with only content expertise receives the highest ratings consistently" (p. 180). Similarly, Feldman (1993) found that years of teaching experience did not affect ratings, supporting the idea that continuous professional development is needed to improve teaching quality and that time on task alone is not sufficient.

The reliability and validity of student ratings has been well established in the literature. As McKeachie (1996) so aptly notes that, "the problem is not in the ratings but in their use" (p. 7). He goes on to say that "often the evaluators give less weight to the student ratings than to less dependable evidence such as peer observations of teaching, testimonials, or general impressions of the teacher's personality" (p. 8). In assessing teaching quality, we need to be cognizant of what ratings are reliable and how they can best be used to improve the quality of teaching. We can make an analogy between student ratings and grading in courses. Too often students' ratings, like grades in courses, are used as labeling devices rather than indicators of areas of strength and weakness. Good teachers know to use tests as tools to help students improve; they give direction regarding content that may need to be repeated or reviewed. The same can be said for student ratings. Like the best teachers, we need to use ratings as indicators of progress and areas needing improvement. Research by Remmers and others has indicated that student ratings do not result in improved teaching quality unless the items are concrete; abstractions have little value in terms of feedback (McKeachie, 1996, p. 5). Nonspecific student ratings are like telling a student that he got a B on an exam without giving the concrete feedback of which items were incorrect. Neither is constructive feedback. Teachers need feedback that provides concrete indicators of where improvement is needed.

More important still is the role of peer review in student ratings. McKeachie et al. (1980) found that improvement was substantial when teachers discussed their ratings with their peers, which leads us to the role of peers in developing teaching quality.

Peer Review Teams

We want to model the best practices in teaching in our own assessment of teaching quality. Typically the review of teaching, particularly that of nontenured faculty members, is conducted separately by faculty peers and by administrators as a means of dual gatekeeping. One of the goals of the learner-centered organization is to break down the historic barrier that divides faculty and administration. Developing a cooperative system for assessing teaching quality provides an opportunity to cross that barrier.

We suggest modeling peer review loosely upon the AQIP accreditation review process, which we mentioned in Chapter 3. The AQIP process is developed around the concept of continuous improvement and peer review and feedback. The basic structure of the AQIP process lends itself nicely to ongoing and long-term assessment of teaching quality.

The first step in the AQIP process involves the institution under review determining its critical characteristics. In other words, what are the defining features that provide a context within which or a background against which the institution should be reviewed? The assessment of teaching quality could begin with the same kind of self-assessment. The teacher being reviewed would ask, What critical characteristics define my course? As we noted earlier in the discussion of teaching philosophy, such characteristics might include the level of course, whether it has prerequisites, and whether it is for majors. These critical characteristics then become contextual keys for reviewers when they look at course design and pedagogical choices.

In the AQIP process, institutions determine areas that provide opportunities for improvement and report on their progress in annual action project reports. These reports are read by trained peers who give constructive feedback on the progress being made. The concept of the peer-reviewed annual progress report also works nicely with assessing teaching effectiveness. Many institutions currently require nontenured as well as tenured faculty to provide annual updates of their teaching, service, and scholarship. The process we envision would include peers, perhaps peers who have identified similar critical characteristics in their own courses, peers who are trained to review reports and give constructive feedback.

The need for training is essential. Just as we would not ask students to evaluate one another's work without providing guidance and practice, we should not operate under the assumption that faculty know how to effectively review one another's teaching without guidance and practice. While colleagues can provide excellent feedback, they are often lenient in their assessments (Centra, 1975). And without guidelines and training for how to give useful feedback, results can be inconsistent among colleagues. Providing direction for reviewers to be more descriptive than evaluative, for example, can elicit more useful feedback for the person being reviewed.

Nearly a decade ago, Nancy Van Note Chism compiled *Peer Review of Teaching* (2007), which can serve as a foundation for exploring peer evaluation of teaching. Her book provides a guide for informed peer judgment and also serves as a source for academic administrators who want to strengthen their system of evaluation. She calls for administrators to make teaching public, to encourage ongoing discussion of teaching, and to be exemplars of thoughtful and informed review of teaching (p. 29). Again we are reminded that academic administrators need to be well informed in order to lead and support the process.

Assessing the Process

Assessment and evaluation drive processes in a learner-centered organization. In regard to the evaluation of faculty in the new paradigm, we will want the mechanisms to focus on learning. In gauging the effectiveness of teaching, students' achievement of learning outcomes will be the major determiner. In gauging the effectiveness of our process of faculty evaluation, the achievement of the faculty members' outcomes will be the major determiner. These two are dependent upon one another. Just as we establish learning outcomes for classes, leaders can set learning outcomes for the quality of teaching at their institutions. We can take the same criteria we use for developing our model for faculty evaluation and apply it to our own work, documenting the results in the leadership portfolio. In our assessment of the faculty evaluation process, we will want to examine the process from the four perspectives recommended by Brookfield (1995), beginning with our self-assessment. To begin the self-assessment, we can simply ask, How have I arranged conditions for learning?

In arranging conditions for learning, we will want to ask what we have done to establish community. Questions might include the following: Am I accessible? Do I convey an enthusiasm, a deep understanding, and a respect for teaching? What have I done to encourage collaboration and cooperation among colleagues, between departments, between institutions? How well do I know the faculty and how well do they know me? Do I share information about myself? What do I do to learn more about the faculty and to engage them in ongoing discussion about teaching?

Do I share power and control? As in the learner-centered class-room, sharing power is not about giving up power, but providing opportunity for making choices. Generally, the evaluation of teaching is a shared process between administration and tenured faculty. What measures have been taken to make this dual evaluation process collaborative rather than independent or even antagonistic, enhancing the formative nature of the process? What kind of process is in place for continuous improvement of tenured faculty teaching? What have I done to create an atmosphere conducive to trusting in the process? What have I done to develop the review process so that peer review is meaningful and substantive?

The self-assessment portion provides one vantage point. In addition, feedback from faculty should be gathered and analyzed as well as feedback from colleagues. And finally, an examination of the literature in relation to faculty evaluation, teaching, and learning should also be included in order to provide multiple viewpoints from which to assess the process.

Modeling a Learner-Centered Approach

A further consideration is the question of how leaders model good teaching in regard to the process of evaluating faculty. As the ones who model the way, leaders will want to analyze the faculty review process in light of learner-centered values, asking the following questions: Does the process show trust in the faculty members being evaluated? Is leadership an expert in the discipline, which in this case is assessment and evaluation of learning? Does leadership create an environment that is conducive to experimentation and risk, including an acceptance of failure? Does leadership demonstrate a belief that good teaching can be learned?

The process for evaluating faculty should reflect the best practices in teaching, the first of which is providing clear and high but attainable expectations. At the point of hire, faculty should be made aware of these expectations along with the supports available to help attain them. Additionally, individuals should have clear and measurable goals. Assessment as well as evaluation, in other words, both formative and summative reviews, should be in place in order to foster a spirit of continuous improvement and engagement in the process. The process should also take into account the individual differences of each person being reviewed, his or her unique journey in achieving authenticity as a teacher. A new faculty member who has never taught, for example, will be less comfortable with experimenting with sharing power and control than the more experienced faculty member who has gained confidence in his or her classroom presence. Authenticity in teaching demands a recognition of the part that individual personality plays in an individual's ability to adopt certain strategies. Growth as a teacher involves continual learning about one's discipline and student learning as well as about one's self. The review process should encourage and foster this learning process. Each institution because of its unique characteristics and mission will develop processes to enhance faculty evaluation; however, regardless of institutional differences, the framework should be dictated by the goals, purpose, and values of the learning paradigm.

Ideally, the process for evaluating learner-centered teaching should reflect the same beliefs about learning that are applied to the student learning environment. These would include active involvement by the learner, or in this case, the teacher; collaboration among peers; a team approach to improved teaching; multiple approaches to assessment that involve the supervising administrator, colleagues, and, of course, the students.

Chapter Summary

Four-Step Process

1. In considering how faculty evaluation is governed by the instructional paradigm, we observed that it is usually a

summative function focusing on the instructor delivering knowledge.

2. In considering how to realign faculty evaluation with the learner-centered paradigm, we offered a method for assessing that is more formative in nature, one that focuses on continuous improvement and does not end with the attainment of tenure.

3. The method is designed around a team approach that asks faculty and administrators together to look at continuous improvement, seeking consistency by asking faculty to consider what the critical characteristics of their courses are and then assessing against those identified qualities.

4. Leaders can model learner-centered practices by creating opportunities for a review process that is a team approach with faculty and administration reviewing in cooperation with an eye for continuous improvement as opposed to assessing against a department norm.

8

Supporting Learning Through
Renovation of Spaces

In the previous chapters we have offered new ways of promoting faculty development centered on teaching effectiveness by fostering community building within units and departments, across disciplines, and throughout individual faculty members' careers. In this final chapter we want to consider the role that physical space plays in learning and subsequently how renovation of spaces can be used to encourage faculty development and learner-centered practices. In Chapter 2 in talking about the rewards of administrative work, we noted that for many administrators, building projects are rewarding because, unlike most of the work we do, the result is something tangible. Building or renovation projects can be exciting and create energy and enthusiasm on a campus. In this chapter we will discuss how we tried to harness the energy and enthusiasm of a renovation project in order to push forward the learner-centered agenda.

Physical Space and Learning

Though we may not be consciously aware of it, physical spaces have a strong effect on learning. While we are usually very aware of how comfort issues—like heat, light, furniture—affect our ability to concentrate, a variety of other factors play a role on the physical nature of the learning environment. On one level, the arrangement of furniture in a classroom can alter the flow of communication and send messages about power and control as well as expectations for learners. On another level, the colors and aesthetics of a room have the power to reinforce learning and encourage participation. As academic leaders responsible for creating and maintaining the physical spaces for teaching, we will want to be aware of these factors so that when we have opportunities to build or renovate, we always place students' learning at the center of the project.

Campus-wide use and arrangement of space, including landscaping and campus symbols, send messages. The distribution of funds for new buildings or renovations also sends messages about institutional priorities. Leadership can sometimes be oblivious to these messages. A colleague told of a campus he visited where the main entrance to the campus had been closed so that guests entered from a hard-to-find side entrance, and a statue of the college founder was situated so that he had his back to the main street in front of the campus. The website for the same institution boasted about its inclusiveness and openness as well as its collaboration with the townspeople. Our colleague found the disconnect between the message sent by the physical landscape and the message on the website remarkable as well as rather amusing.

We have focused on the need for leadership to be intentional in realigning institutional policies and procedures with the learner-centered paradigm. Equally important is an intentional focus on the physical campus and the messages it sends about priorities and institutional values. Thomas Fisher (2007), dean of the College of Design at the University of Minnesota–Twin Cities, commented in a roundtable discussion of campus sustainability: "I think campuses are headed not so much to a cliff but toward a brick wall. Tuition has risen far faster than inflation. . . . We are going to be less affluent in this country, and our institutions are going to be less affluent. And what I hope comes from that is not just trying to maintain the old paradigm and watch everything slowly decay, but that we actually go through the paradigm shift and fundamentally operate in different ways—a sort of rediscovering of what we are"

(p. B19). As we lead the shift into the new paradigm, we will be called upon to reconsider our physical environment as well.

Some have posited that the brick-and-mortar university will become obsolete as we move into an online educational environment. That reality is unlikely. The *Chronicle of Higher Education* annually features new architecture on campuses that illustrates the millions of dollars colleges and universities are investing in a physical presence, many using the opportunity to lead the way in sustainable construction and eco-friendly architecture. As our precarious economy continues to affect our budgeting in profound ways, even more care will need to be taken when investing in bricks and mortar, with thought to the symbolic use of those investments as well as thought for this undefined future. Additionally, we argue that as we modify our traditional campuses in order to be responsive to the changing environment of higher education, we must do so with awareness of what we know about the generation of students now entering college and how they learn (Harris & Cullen, 2007).

As we develop a new paradigm of the physical campus and where students learn, we need to rethink our conception of learning spaces and our use of space, both in terms of pedagogy and sustainability. Architect Steven Bingler in "Less Is More: Learning Environments for the Next Century" (2007), states, "There are other imperatives for exploring the development of more expansive environments for learning. One of the most compelling is that we can no longer afford to build and rebuild the stand-alone physical infrastructure that has characterized factory model schools of the twentieth century" (pp. 1–2). He suggests that the frugality that institutions must face in maintaining the physical campus can be an opportunity for innovation as we dispense with the stand-alone model and seek flexible environments that are "integrated, energizing, cooperative, and efficient" (p. 2). While maintaining accountability in terms of student learning outcomes, we must also remain accountable for the funds, both public and private, that support our physical environment.

Seeing the Influence of the Instructional Paradigm

When we hear the word *classroom*, most likely the image that first comes to mind is a room with tablet armchairs all facing the front of the room, where a teacher's desk is located in front of, depending upon your age, a black or green chalkboard or a whiteboard. This classroom configuration and large lecture halls with fixed seating were the most practical and conducive for transferring information from professor to student. If the model for teaching was for professors to transmit information to recipient students, then it only made sense to have the professor as the central point of interest in the front of the room with a variety of aids for transmitting information: blackboard or whiteboard, overhead projector, television monitors. White (1990) noted that the configuration of the traditional rectangular classroom with seats in rows often attached to the floor was influenced by the architectural style of the early twentieth century.

This configuration limits and even discourages interaction among students because the communication pattern that is created by this arrangement is between professor and student, most often in one direction, professor to student. White (1990) wrote that "classroom seating patterns are central to the notion of improving communication within the classroom both from a student-teacher standpoint as well as that between students. Extensive research strongly suggests that student communication has a direct correlation with students' placement within the room" (p. 4). The traditional configuration is also reflective of the instructional paradigm as competition-based, each student competing with one another for the approval (aka grade) of the teacher who directs and controls learning within the environment.

Typically classroom and laboratory spaces are segregated by college and department. The separation and "ownership" of space reflects the silo effect of the instructional paradigm. Furthermore, the allocation of resources for maintaining these silos is indicative of institutional values. A recent commentary in the *Chronicle of*

Higher Education by a student from an East Coast university is titled "A Student's View: Invest in People, Not Buildings" (Jones, 2008). The student comments on the allocation of resources that betrays the true values of her institution.

In the race to lure students to campuses, many academic leaders focus on student unions and recreation facilities, assuming that students as traditional-aged freshmen will choose the school with the best recreation facilities. However, the opinion of the student in the *Chronicle of Higher Education* as well as other students surveyed reveals that the most important factor regarding campus facilities in students' choice of an institution is the support of infrastructure related to the students' academic major, followed by the quality of the library. This preference is most likely caused by changing demographics whereby more and more students are older, have families, and full work schedules; for them, campus recreation facilities are of little importance. Additionally, the cost of attending college has not only forced more and more students to work full time, but also to reassess priorities, and the quality of the education in their major is still the main reason for attending college.

Realigning with the New Paradigm

We have repeated the point that the learner-centered paradigm is built upon recent and emerging research on how people learn. A considerable body of research is also available on how physical environment affects learning. At this time when we are being challenged to rethink our curricula and to reexamine what it means to educate students, recent research on how students learn should inform our decision-making. As we struggle to shift toward a learning-centered academic environment that fosters collaborative, active engagement on the part of the student and a more facilitative role for the professor, our needs in terms of physical spaces must necessarily shift also. As we expect students to engage in learning activities that take place outside the classroom, we need to consider how space functions to support that goal by reenvisioning the entire campus as a learning space.

In his 1995 text *Brain-Based Learning*, Eric Jensen examined optimal environments for learning. He explained that 80–90 percent of all information absorbed by the brain is visual (p. 55). Among the visual elements that affect us so strongly is color. According to Jensen (1995), "Color has impact because it is part of the spectrum of electromagnetic radiation" (p. 56). He cites Robert Gerard of the University of California stating that every color has a wavelength and every wavelength affects the brain differently. Engelbrecht (2003) wrote that "color elicits a total response from human beings because the energy produced by the light that carries color affects our body functions and influences our mind and emotion" (p. 1). She reported that studies have indicated that color can affect attention span, eyestrain, work productivity, and accuracy. Selection of color is not only a matter of hue but also intensity of color and contrast; monotone environments may induce anxiety and lead to irritability and an inability to concentrate. White (1990) also noted that classroom color has been recognized as a major factor in classroom environment. He quotes James Thompson (1973): "Color is a silent language, a unique and subtle symbol system used by humans, consciously and subconsciously, to send each other information" (p. 5). White concluded that the mental stimulation students passively receive as a result of the color in a room helps both the student and teacher stay focused. It is important for additional research to be conducted on color in educational environments.

In addition to color, Jensen (1995) also discusses the unconscious effect of items of visual interest, items he labels *peripherals*. "Peripherals in the form of positive affirmations, learner-generated work, images depicting change, growth, beauty can be powerful vehicles of expression" (p. 59). In other words, the aesthetics of a space play a role in the receptivity of the learner. The visual presentation of the classroom makes a subconscious statement to the student about learning and how learning will occur in the space.

We have emphasized the point that in the learner-centered paradigm, teaching is about making conscious choices in selecting effective practices for teaching, recognizing the interrelationship among curriculum design, assessment, learning practices, facilitation, and learning environment. The concept that classroom arrangement affects learning is not new. Numerous researchers (Sommer, 1977; Anderson, 1971; Haney & Zimbardo, 1975; Hennings, 1975) have written about classroom design on learning. Weinstein and Woolfolk (1981), recognizing the symbolic impact of classroom arrangement, wrote, "The visual appearance of the classroom can be conceptualized as a nonverbal statement about the teacher who has structured this learning environment" (p. 383). One of those choices is seating arrangement, which sends subconscious signals to students about learning and affects patterns of communication.

One of the key features of the learner-centered approach to teaching is recognition of the role of students' prior learning on their ability or willingness to learn new things. Prior learning plays an important role in room arrangement as well. As with other external stimuli, the arrangement of the furniture in the classroom sends an unspoken message to the students based upon their prior knowledge.

The three seating options pictured in Figures 8.1, 8.2, and 8.3 send different messages to students regarding their role as learner, and each fosters a different communication pattern in the classroom.

The seating pattern in Figure 8.1 is used in cinemas, theaters, churches, and lecture halls. In each of these contexts, the social norm is to be passive and receptive, so when students enter a classroom set up in this style, they rightly expect to be acted upon, to receive information, or even to be entertained.

The seminar seating pattern in Figure 8.2 exposes the student, in contrast to the anonymity of lecture hall seating, where the student is one in a mass audience. The student is held more accountable by the teacher in this setting where there is no one to hide behind

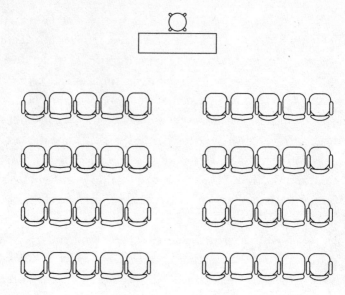

Figure 8.1

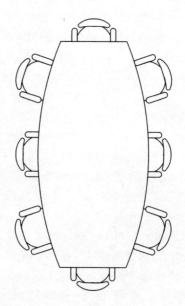

Figure 8.2

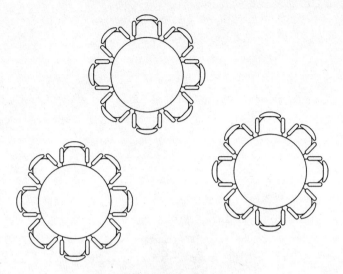

Figure 8.3

as in auditorium-style seating, but the communication pattern is still teacher directed. The contextual references that influence the student's expectations for learning are formal, such as a board room or formal dining room, settings in which a clear hierarchy exists in relation to seating position around the table. This seating pattern is more conducive to discussion than the lecture hall; however, the teacher still retains prominence in the pattern of communication.

The module style seating in Figure 8.3 greatly increases opportunities for student engagement and reduces the role of the teacher in relation to the communication pattern. When individuals sit in small groups, interchange and conversation are expected. The contextual references the students bring to this configuration are circumstances that encourage, even demand, interaction, such as eating a casual meal or playing a game. For an individual to sit passively in receiver mode in these social situations would be inappropriate and perhaps considered rude by other participants. When a student enters a classroom set up in this configuration, the student expects to participate.

Cooperative learning is a strategy used to promote engagement through increasing interaction among learners. Seating patterns can either encourage or stifle interaction in these circumstances. Auditorium-style seating patterns decrease communication among participants, placing the teacher in the pivotal position of controlling discussion, whereas seating arrangements that deemphasize the teacher as controller of communication promote the desired outcome of these learning strategies.

In *The Importance of Physical Space in Creating Supportive Learning Environments* (Chism & Bickford, 2002), Nancy Chism writes, "We know too much about how learning occurs to continue to ignore the ways in which learning spaces are planned, constructed and maintained" (p. 5). But in truth we have been ignoring research on the effects of the physical aspects of the classroom for decades. Most of what the past three decades of literature have called for is open, well-lighted, flexible spaces with comfortable furnishings. Yet if we look at most college classrooms, they do not conform. Predominantly we see large lecture halls with fixed seating, smaller classrooms with tablet armchairs or tables and chairs all facing a defined front of the classroom. We see a clear delineation between teacher space and student space. What we see are the vestiges of the instructional paradigm.

Diana Oblinger (2000), in writing about space as an agent of change, states that "space can bring people together; it can encourage exploration, collaboration, and discussion. Or, space can carry an unspoken message of silence and disconnectedness" (p. 1.1). She defines *built pedagogy* as "the ability of space to define how one teaches." Too often our limited options regarding classroom arrangement dictate pedagogical options.

Assessing the Process

Assessment can play an important role in maximizing the effect of room or building renovation. Assessment can be used to gain necessary feedback on the process as well as to gain buy-in and engagement in the enterprise from the entire community.

Utilization of space is both a matter of fiscal concern and another way of looking at sustainability, which is a major concern in renovation projects. In addition to the Leadership in Energy and Environmental Design (LEED) *whole building* focus on sustainability, we also consider room utilization as a factor, a way of maximizing efficiency of space after construction. One of the features of the instructional paradigm is fragmentation, illustrated visibly in the silos that develop around departmental and college territories. Many campuses suffer from underutilized spaces as a result of territoriality. We conducted a review of space utilization on our campus and found that a majority of spaces were underutilized. Yet we knew that during a renovation project that caused the simultaneous closure of two of the major classroom buildings, the campus was still able to provide all the needed classroom space, a phenomenon that pointed to the problem of territoriality. Space was abundant; sharing was not.

In considering our use of space, we also conducted an assessment of our existing classrooms. We developed a rubric based on criteria gleaned from the past three decades of research on the effect of physical space on receptivity to learning as well as the wealth of research on cognition and learning. We used this rubric to make initial assessments of the spaces.

This assessment revealed predominantly large lecture halls with fixed seating and smaller classrooms with tablet armchairs or tables and chairs all facing a defined front of the classroom. We found a clear delineation between teacher space and student space. The overall aesthetic was "institutional," white floors and walls, black or green chalkboards providing the only color, and more often than not, furniture that was not accommodating to a variety of body types. Lighting was also poor, because of old fixtures, dated window treatments, and in most cases an inconsistency in light bulbs which cast a disconcerting array of light in a single area. From this initial assessment we began working with professional design services to transform these areas to learner-centered spaces as defined in the criteria of our rubric.

This assessment led to the renovation of nearly fifty classrooms, a project that was conducted in several phases in order to allow us to continue to assess the effects of the renovations on the ultimate goal of fostering learner-centered pedagogy. We began by renovating ten highly used classrooms. We chose classrooms based upon the number of different classes and professors who used the rooms in order to reach a wide variety of users. Satisfaction surveys were given to all faculty and students who used these rooms.

The survey responses yielded important results. The criteria on our rubric appeared to be valid; however, while there was overall satisfaction on the part of faculty and students, there did not appear to be significant changes taking place in pedagogy. Our faculty members were not as prepared as we had thought in terms of transforming their pedagogy. For example, simply providing moveable furnishings and technology in the rooms did not necessarily inspire the faculty to move the furniture or use the technology. The faculty members were responding to the rooms from a very practical perspective based upon an established mode of instruction.

The assessment of the new classrooms guided our faculty development efforts through our Faculty Center, which took place simultaneously with the renovation of existing classrooms. Throughout the multistage process, we continued renovating existing classroom spaces, surveying faculty, and reassessing our design and technology choices based on feedback, thus gaining buy-in and ownership from all involved.

Changing a culture requires buy-in, engagement, and intellectual investment, which, in this case, we gained through the process of ongoing assessment. The point of assessment was not solely to gain feedback as we proceeded through the stages of this project; the ongoing assessment empowered the community, involved them in the process, and most importantly, sparked a campus-wide discussion, not just about space, but about learning and what it means to be a learning-centered campus.

Modeling a Learner-Centered Approach

In modeling the way, our aim is to make visible the change we are trying to effect. There may be no better opportunity to do so than in the remodeling of physical spaces. Renovation and/or building projects provide us the opportunity to make our buildings define, in a physical way, our mission of becoming a learning-centered academic environment. Modeling the way in regard to physical spaces for learning can take three dimensions: (1) supporting renovation of existing spaces and creation of new spaces to support learning; (2) prioritizing allocation of resources to best support learning inside and outside of the classroom; and (3) fostering community, team work, collaboration across disciplines through careful planning of new structures and encouraging less ownership of space by discipline through the design of interdisciplinary spaces.

As an example of modeling the way in regard to physical spaces and learning, we made a comprehensive effort to transform learning and spaces for learning in order to change the cultural paradigm. We undertook a multistage project to renovate learning spaces in a systematic fashion, combining assessment and development for both faculty and administrators in order to maximize our efforts to transform the academic milieu, both physically and intellectually (Harris & Cullen, 2007).

This project involved multiple stages, beginning with the renovation of classrooms we described in the section on assessment. This cosmetic renovation process allowed us to develop a classroom template and to arrive at standards for technology, furniture options, and color palette.

The follow-up to the classroom renovation project involved the renovation of a classroom building. Typically in public universities, buildings are built and later renovated by appropriations from the state, in the name of capital outlay funds. The capital outlay funding for this renovation project was minimal and came to us with no greater expectation on the part of the state or campus leadership than a physical upgrade of the building. However, we used this opportunity to intentionally make visible our mission to become learning-centered. The symbolic impact of the renovation worked in our favor.

The capital outlay renovation project was directed toward a building that had been constructed in 1969 and at the time was considered state of the art. Ironically, its name was the Instructional Resource Center (IRC). The IRC was divided into an instructional wing comprised of four large tiered auditoria and a two-story wing for studios, offices, and other spaces. Built with a focus on instruction, delivery of content, the 150- and 200-seat auditoria were furnished with large rear-projection screens and audiovisual equipment designed to disseminate information to large numbers of students. In order to capitalize on the symbolism, we renamed the building the Interdisciplinary Resource Center. The renovation project sought to create a space that would focus on learning: fostering a variety of teaching methods and learning styles, enhancing learning inside and outside the classroom, encouraging learning through teamwork and interaction, facilitating learning through the use of technology, and creating interdisciplinary learning environments that facilitate inclusion and engagement.

The initial classroom renovations provided us with useful information regarding faculty and student preferences for furniture, use of color, carpeting options, and placement of technology in classrooms. However, this time we were not constrained by the shape and size of existing spaces, which allowed us far greater opportunity to innovate, making a conscious effort to create spaces that reflected the research.

A key feature of our project was the role the Faculty Center would play in the development of the spaces and, even more, in the future use of the facility. In order to capitalize on the role that the

Faculty Center would play, we physically moved the Faculty Center from its location in the library to the renovated building, replicating the offices and existing training spaces and adding enhancements, our way of emphasizing that faculty development was both literally and figuratively the driving force in effecting change. The new site for the Center increased the sense of the Center as a safe place for faculty because the location, while central to the campus, was more private and afforded space not only for confidential interchange but also room for experimentation and practice. The new classrooms were designed to be used by faculty from all disciplines, with priority given to those who were experimenting with new techniques, team teaching, or conducting research on innovation.

In order to achieve the goal of flexible spaces, we flattened the floors of the auditoria to create spaces that could accommodate moveable furnishings. Unlike the traditional rectangular classroom, the new classrooms each had an unusual shape that virtually precluded an obvious *front* of the classroom, thus minimizing the sense of teacher space. We used tables with multiple folding options and chairs with casters to promote ease of movement. Each space was carpeted, comfortable, colorful, and technologically advanced.

A major feature was the inclusion of "spill-out" spaces for students, both private student gathering rooms directly outside the classrooms and a connector space of approximately 6,000 square feet linking the building to the adjacent building and providing a study area, flexible gathering area, and a main pathway for connecting west and east campus.

The interior of the connector space was designed to be a comfortable and aesthetically pleasing work environment. We incorporated a post-and-beam system which provided an implied boundary within the large open space, encouraging collaboration and supporting technology integration. A coffeehouse area and a parklike environment with trees and other natural elements added to the informal nature of the space. In an effort to take advantage of the research on the effects of color and light, the design maximized the available natural light with exposure from east, west, and north. We wanted to keep elements natural yet incorporate the spectrum of color that is supposed to most greatly enhance learning: orange and buff. Therefore we chose a terra cotta and buff tile for the flooring and terra cotta brick. Throughout the design and construction phases of the project, the Faculty Center continued its intense development programming for both faculty and administrators, facilitating learning communities on topics related to learner-centered teaching prior to the opening of the new spaces.

The most significant lesson learned from our multistage renovation projects was that to achieve the goal of a learner-centered curriculum, changing the physical spaces is a necessary condition but not a sufficient one. Changing a culture requires buy-in, engagement, and intellectual investment, which, in this case, we attempted to gain through the process of ongoing development and assessment.

The transformation of learning spaces provided a physical manifestation of the cultural shift that we initiated. We believe that through this project we facilitated a strategic step in the process of transforming our campus, both physically and intellectually, toward a learner-centered focus.

The Leadership Portfolio

In the preface, we made reference to an anachronistic paradigm that dominates our thinking and subsequently makes bringing about change extremely difficult. If we are to effectively bring about a shift to a new paradigm, one that fosters community, one that breaks down the silos, divisiveness and fragmentation, we will need physical spaces that reflect that goal, for as Winston Churchill stated, "We shape our buildings, and afterwards our buildings shape us."

Throughout we have stressed the need for intentionality, for deliberate and conscious attention to all our decisions so that they support and push forward the new paradigm. The leadership portfolio is a place to document that thinking and planning in regard to physical spaces for learning. Leaders will want to document in the portfolio and in other public statements the larger goals of renovation projects, such as fostering community, interdisciplinary learning and scholarship, adaptability and cooperation. Building and renovation for the new paradigm will call for shared spaces, rooms that can be reconfigured, furnishings that accommodate the vast and varied population of learners and learning styles who belong to our community. Building and renovation is about more than simply beautifying a campus. Through these projects, we have the opportunity to create the physical manifestation of the paradigm we seek.

Chapter Summary

- In considering how room renovation is governed by the instructional paradigm, we observed that the traditional classroom reflects the factory model of education and is designed for the transmittal of knowledge.

- In considering how to realign room renovation with the learner-centered paradigm, we observed that spaces for learning need to be flexible, offer opportunities for team work and collaboration as well as spill-out spaces where learning can continue beyond the confines of the classroom.

- The method we described was a renovation project which incorporated assessment throughout the process not only to gain information on room usability but, more important, to engage the community in the process in order to help drive change.

- Leaders can model learner-centered practices by creating opportunities to engage the entire campus community in renovation of learning spaces, using the opportunity to push forward the learner-centered agenda.

Closing Thoughts

We began by examining the current pressures upon higher education which make this the time for change. We then examined the paradigm that currently governs our work, the instructional paradigm that fosters isolation, unhealthy competition, divisiveness between administration and faculty, and organizational fragmentation. Because of the overriding mechanistic view of learning that underpins thinking in this paradigm, dualistic thinking and technical problem solving predominate, neither of which will foster change. We posited that in order to effectively change higher education, we must change the paradigm that governs our thinking.

This is, of course, a tall order because as humans we fear the unknown; it is our nature to resist change. In order to motivate change, people need to have a goal, a vision, to know where they are headed. In Chapter 3 we looked at the learner-centered paradigm as the goal of the proposed change. We examined the learner-centered classroom in light of the major changes in practice that learner-centered teachers adopt and then considered the administrative applications of these same practices. Then in Chapter 4, we considered the leadership skills necessary to bring about this change, again comparing the similarities between good teaching and good leading, noting the common characteristics of competence, vision, and the ability to motivate. To develop the leadership skills that individuals will need to lead the way to the new paradigm, leaders can assume the role of learner-centered teacher, the guides who will empower those around them to reach their goal.

Part I offered a framework for conceptualizing change, an outline of approaches for leaders to apply in order to foster the shift to the new paradigm. In Part II, we presented examples of strategies that we used in trying to push forward the learner-centered agenda. We showed how faculty evaluation could be transformed to be a process for continuous improvement, and we also introduced a means for fostering professional development based upon data gleaned from course syllabi. We described an orientation program for new faculty that builds community and cultivates collaboration and cross-disciplinary support, and we discussed the importance of physical spaces on learning and showed how a capital outlay renovation project was used to advance the learner-centered agenda. These examples were not meant as a prescription or formula but as illustrations of practices that were successful for us. We offered these as examples of modeling the way, showing how we attempted to realign our practices with the new paradigm and to use assessment as a driver of change.

Leading the learner-centered campus will involve a considerable amount of personal challenge along with the more obvious institutional challenges that will abound, for the journey is both personal and institutional. In considering how as individuals we have been molded by the instructional paradigm, we may find ourselves questioning very fundamental beliefs that we have held fast to or beliefs that we considered to be so true that we never challenged their authenticity. Like children who have been raised in a rigid patriarchal family and are first exposed to families where father is not the sole authority, we will experience transformative events that will lead us to question beliefs we have held as norms. And once we begin questioning one assumption, we will begin questioning others, which can lead to insecurity and doubt. This journey will take strength of character, resolve to succeed, and enduring optimism.

Although we have emphasized the need for self-reflection and self-assessment, particularly in regard to the leader portfolio, we want to clarify that leading the learner-centered campus is not a solo task. While self-assessment is an important element, leading is a collaborative venture. Leading the learner-centered campus presents leaders with new challenges. In the preceding chapters we have attempted to provide a guide for leaders to examine the role of leadership in the learner-centered institution and to provide some guidelines as well as specific illustrations of strategies for pushing forward the learner-centered agenda. We likened the process of making this shift to learning a second language. Certain parts of language use come more easily than others, and different learners excel in different areas. We begin our language learning always in a state of translation, making references to our first language in order to put the pieces together, but once we achieve proficiency, we stop translating and start thinking in the new language.

In practicing speaking in a new language, it is always advised to converse with more advanced speakers. While a country full of native speakers of the learner-centered paradigm may not be available to us for a total immersion experience, there are certainly those who are more advanced in their language learning. John Tagg's *The Learning Paradigm College* (2003) provides numerous examples of institutions that are making positive changes toward achieving the goal. Conversation with these institutions would certainly enhance our language learning.

Achieving proficiency takes time, takes practice, and involves making a lot of mistakes. The guide we have provided is based upon this concept. The first step in examining our practices and processes is one of translation, looking at how we spoke in the instructional paradigm and how we will now speak in the learner-centered one. As we repeat this translation process, working systematically through our institutional practices, we will become more proficient, expand our vocabulary, and become more at ease and confident. Eventually we will not need to translate anymore. We will begin to think in the new language, to think in the new paradigm.

The well-known quotation by Mahatma Gandhi "You must become the change you wish to see in the world" expresses the simple yet profound nature of change. In the preceding chapters we have made the case for the need for change in higher education if we are to weather the storm of forces affecting our work. We have focused on the role of leadership in effecting change and offered a means of systematically fostering the shift from the instructional paradigm to the learner-centered paradigm. What we have offered, which we believe sets this volume apart from others, is an examination of the comprehensive nature of the solution. At the heart of that solution, though, lies the greatest challenge, which is the personal nature of change required of individuals. Changing paradigms means changing worldviews, changing habits, changing ourselves. We have made the point that our institutions are a result of the human interactions that take place within them. Institutions cannot change without the people who constitute them changing first. If we are to become the world we wish to see, then we must practice living as if that world exists. The paradigm will not shift until individuals begin living as if it already had.

Leaders of this change will be challenged to inspire, to foster hope, anticipation, and excitement over the prospect of the birth of a new paradigm. It is our hope that this book will serve as a useful guide to those who are willing to rise to the challenge of leading the learner-centered campus.

References

Acker, J. (1990). Hierarchies, jobs, bodies: A theory of gendered organizations. *Gender and Society, 4,* 139–158.

American Association of University Professors. (2008). *The annual report on the economic status of the profession, 2007–08.* Retrieved from http://www.aaup.org/AAUP/pubsres/academe/2008/MA/sal/sal.htm.

American Psychological Association. (2008). *Learner-centered psychological principles.* Retrieved from http://www.apa.org/ed/lcp2/lcp14.html.

Amey, M. J. (1996). The institutional marketplace and faculty attrition. *Thought & Action, 12*(1), 235.

Anderson, E. L. (2002). *The new professoriate: Characteristics, contributions, and compensation.* Washington, DC: American Council on Education.

Anderson, R. (1971). The school as an organic teaching aid. In R. M. McClure (Ed.), *National society for the study of education yearbook, Part 1. The curriculum: Retrospect and prospect* (pp. 271–306). Chicago: University of Chicago Press.

Argyris, C. (1993, October). Beware of skilled incompetence. *R & D Innovator, 2*(10). Retrieved from http://www.winstonbrill.com/bril001/html/article_index/articles51_100.html.

Arreola, R. (2007). *Developing a comprehensive faculty evaluation system: A guide to designing, building, and operating large-scale evaluation systems.* San Francisco: Jossey-Bass.

Ayers, W. (1986). Thinking about teachers and the curriculum. *Harvard Educational Review, 56*(1), 49–51.

Bain, K. (2004). *What the best college teachers do.* Cambridge, MA: Harvard University Press.

Baldwin, R. G., & Chronister, J. (2002). *Teaching without tenure: Policies and practices for a new era.* Baltimore: Johns Hopkins University Press.

Bandura, A. (1986). *Social foundations of thought and action: A social cognitive theory.* Englewood Cliffs, NJ: Prentice Hall.

Bandura, A. (1993). Perceived self-efficacy in cognitive development and functioning. *Educational Psychologist, 28,* 117–48.

Bandura, A. (1994). Self-efficacy. In *Encyclopedia of human behavior* (Vol. 4, pp. 71–81). New York: Academic Press.

Bandura, A. (1997). *Self-efficacy: The exercise of control.* New York: Freeman.

Banks, W. M. (1984). Afro-American scholars in the university. *American Behavioral Scientist, 27*(3), 325–338.

Barr, R., & Tagg, J. (1995). From teaching to learning: A new paradigm for undergraduate education. *Change Magazine, 27*(6), 13–25.

Beaudoin, M. (1998). *A new professoriate for the new millennium.* Retrieved from http://www.edgecombe.cc.nc.us/ECC_DOCS/Changing.HTM.

Beaudry, M., & Schaub, T. (1998). The learning-centered syllabus. *The Teaching Professor, 12,* 2–3.

Bensimon, E. M., & Neumann, A. (1993). *Redesigning collegiate leadership: Teams and teamwork in higher education.* Baltimore: Johns Hopkins University Press.

Biggs, J. (1999). *Teaching for quality learning at university: What the student does.* Buckingham, UK: Society for Research into Higher Education and Open University Press.

Bingler, S. (2007). Less is more: Learning environments for the next century. *New Horizons for Learning.* Retrieved from http://www.newhorizons.org/strategies/learning_environments/bingler.htm.

Blackburn, R. T., & Bentley, R. J. (1993). Faculty research productivity: Some moderators of associated stressors. *Research in Higher Education, 34*(6), 725–745.

Blackburn, R. T., & Lawrence, J. H. (1995). *Faculty at work: Motivation, expectation, satisfaction.* Baltimore: Johns Hopkins University Press.

Boice, R. (1992). *The new faculty member: Supporting and fostering professional development.* San Francisco: Jossey-Bass.

Bok, D. (2005). *Our underachieving colleges: A candid look at how much students learn and why they should be learning more.* Princeton, NJ: Princeton University Press.

Bolman, L. G., & Deal, T. E. (2008). *Reframing organizations: Artistry choice and leadership.* San Francisco: Jossey-Bass.

Bowden, J., & Marton, F. (1998). *The university of learning.* London, UK: Kogan Page.

Braskamp, L., & Ory, J. (1994). *Assessing faculty work.* San Francisco: Jossey-Bass.

Brookfield, S. (1995). *Becoming a critically reflective teacher.* San Francisco: Jossey-Bass.

Brookfield, S. (2006). *The skillful teacher: On trust, technique, and responsiveness in the classroom.* San Francisco: Jossey-Bass.

Brookfield, S., Kalliath, T., & Laiken, M. (2006). Exploring the connections between adult and management education. *Journal of Management Education, 30*(6), 828–839.

Bruffee, K. A. (1993). *Collaborative learning: Higher education interdependence and the authority of knowledge.* Baltimore: Johns Hopkins University Press.

Bruner, J. S. (1971). *The relevance of education.* New York: W. W. Norton.

Bruner, J. S. (1973). *Beyond the information given: Studies in the psychology of knowing.* New York: W. W. Norton.

Burns, J. M. (1978). *Leadership.* New York: Harper & Row.

Carlson, C. R., & Wilmot, W. W. (2006). *Innovation: The five disciplines for creating what customers want.* San Francisco: Jossey-Bass.

Cashin, W. E. (1990). Students do rate different academic fields differently. In M. Theall & J. Franklin (Eds.), *New Directions for Teaching and Learning, No. 43. Student ratings of instruction: Issues for improving practice* (pp. 113–121). San Francisco: Jossey-Bass.

Centra, J. A. (1975). Colleagues as raters of classroom instruction. *Journal of Higher Education, 46,* 327–337.

Centra, J. A. (1979). *Determining faculty effectiveness.* San Francisco: Jossey-Bass.

Centra, J. A. (1993). *Reflective faculty evaluation.* San Francisco: Jossey-Bass.

Chickering, A. (2000, March). Creating community within individual courses. In B. Jacoby & Associates (Eds.), *New Directions for Higher Education, No. 109. Involving commuter students in learning* (pp. 23–32). San Francisco: Jossey-Bass.

Chickering, A., & Gamson, Z. (1987, March). Seven principles for good practice in undergraduate education. *AAHE Bulletin, 39*(7), 3–7.

Chism, N. V. N. (1998). Developing a philosophy of teaching statement. In E. O. Chandler (Ed.), *Essays on teaching excellence, 1997–1998 series.* Nederland, CO: Professional and Organizational Development Network in Higher Education. Retrieved from http://www.cofc.edu/~cetl/Essays/DevelopingaPhilosophyofTeaching.html.

Chism, N. V. N. (2007). *Peer review of teaching: A sourcebook* (2nd ed.). San Francisco: Jossey-Bass.

Chism, N. V. N., & Bickford, D. (Eds.). (2002). *The importance of physical space in creating learning environments.* San Francisco: Jossey-Bass.

Chliwiniak, L. (1997). *Higher education leadership: Analyzing the gender gap. ASHE-ERIC Higher Education Report, 25:4.* Washington, DC: The George Washington University, Graduate School of Education and Human Development.

Collay, M. (2002). Balancing work and family. In J. E. Cooper & D. D. Stevens (Eds.), *Tenure in the sacred grove: Issues and strategies for women and minority faculty* (pp. 89–106). Albany, NY: SUNY Press.

Collins, J. (2001). *Good to great.* New York: Harper Business.

Conway, M., Perfect, T., Anderson, W., Gardiner, J., & Cohen, G. (1997). Changes in memory awareness during learning: The acquisition of knowledge by psychology undergraduates. *Journal of Experimental Psychology: General, 126*(4), 393–413.

Cooper, J. E., & Stevens, D. D. (Eds.). (2002). *Tenure in the sacred grove: Issues and strategies for women and minority faculty.* Albany, NY: SUNY Press.

Copur, H. (1990). Academic professionals: A study of conflict and satisfaction in the professoriate. *Human Relations, 43*(2), 113–127.

Covey, S. (1989). *Seven habits of highly effective people.* New York: Free Press.

Covington, M. (1992). *Making the grade: A self-worth perspective on motivation and school reform.* New York: Cambridge University Press.

Cox, M. D. (2004). Introduction to faculty learning communities. In M. D. Cox & L. Richlin (Eds.), *New Directions for Teaching and Learning, No. 97. Building faculty learning communities* (pp. 5–25). San Francisco: Jossey-Bass.

Cox, M. D., & Richlin, L. (Eds.). (2004). *New Directions for Teaching and Learning, No. 97. Building faculty learning communities.* San Francisco: Jossey-Bass.

Cranton, P. (2004). Perspectives on authenticity in teaching. *Adult Education Quarterly, 55*(5), 5–22.

Cranton, P. (2006). *Understanding and promoting transformative learning: A guide for educators of adults.* San Francisco: Jossey-Bass.

Crutcher, R., O'Brien, P., Corigan, R., & Schneider, C. (2007). *College learning for the new global century: A report from the National Leadership Council for Liberal Education and America's Promise.* Washington, DC: American Association of State Colleges and Universities.

Csikszentmihalyi, M. (1990). *Flow: The psychology of optimal experience.* New York: Harper & Row.

Cullen, R. (2007). The rewards of our work. *Academic Leader, 23*(12), 1–2.

Cullen, R., & Harris, M. (2008). Renovation as innovation: Transforming a campus symbol and a campus culture. *Perspectives: Policy and Practice in Higher Education, 12*(1), 47–51.

Cullen, R., & Harris, M. (2009). Assessing learning-centeredness. *Assessment and Evaluation in Higher Education, 34*(1), 115–125. doi:10.1080/02602930801956018

Currie, J., Thiele, B., & Harris, P. (2002). *Gendered universities in globalized economies: Power careers, and sacrifices.* New York: Lexington Books.

Davis, J. (2003). *Learning to lead: A handbook for postsecondary administrators.* Westport, CT: American Council on Education & Praeger.

de la Luz Reyes, M., & Halcon, J. J. (1988). Racism in academia: The old wolf revisited. *Harvard Educational Review, 58*(3), 299–314.

Demott, J. (1987, February 23). Welcome America to the baby bust. *Time.* Retrieved from www.time.com/time/arts/article/0,8599,1731528,00 .html?imw=Y.

Dever, J. T. (1997). Reconciling educational leadership and the learning organization. *Community College Review, 25*(2), 57–63.

DeVries, D. L. (1975). The relationship of role expectations on faculty behavior. *Research in Higher Education, 3,* 111–129.

Dewey, J. (1933). *How we think.* Lexington, MA: Heath.

Diamond, R. M., Gardiner, L. F., & Wheeler, D. W. (2002). Requisites for sustainable institutional change. In R. M. Diamond (Ed.), *Field guide to academic leadership* (pp. 15–26). San Francisco: Jossey-Bass.

Dolence, M., & Norris, D. (1995). *Transforming higher education: A vision for learning in the 21st century.* Ann Arbor, MI: Society for College and University Planning.

Driscoll, J. W. (1978). Trust and participation in organizational decision making as predictors of satisfaction. *The Academy of Management Journal, 21*(1), 44–56.

Drucker, P. (2002, August). The discipline of innovation. *Harvard Review,* 95–104.

Dweck, C. (2000). *Self-theories: Their role in motivation, personality, and development.* Philadelphia: Psychology Press.

Dweck, C. (2006). *Mindsets: The new psychology of success.* New York: Random House.

Dweck, C., & Licht, C. (1980). Learned helplessness and intellectual achievement. In J. Gerber & M. E. P. Seligman (Eds.), *Human helplessness theory and application* (pp. 197–221). New York: Academic Press.

Eddy, P. L., & VanderLinden, K. E. (2006). Emerging definitions of leadership in higher education: New visions of leadership or same old "hero" leader? *Community College Review, 34*(1), 5–26.

Eisner, E. W. (1983). The art and craft of teaching. *Education Leadership, 40*(4), 5–13.

Engelbrecht, K. (2003, June 18). *The impact of color on learning.* Presentation at NeoCon® 2003. Retrieved from http://www.coe.uga.edu/sdpl/HTML/W305.pdf.

Entwistle, N., & Entwistle, A. (1991). Contrasting forms of understanding for degree examinations: The student experience and its implications. *Higher Education, 22*, 205–227.

Fairweather, J. (2006). *Faculty work and public trust.* Boston: Allyn and Bacon.

Farnsworth, K. (2007). *Leadership as service.* Westport, CT: Praeger.

Feldman, K. A. (1978). Course characteristics and college students' ratings of their teacher: What we know and what we don't. *Research in Higher Education, 9*, 199–242.

Feldman, K. A. (1993). College students' views of male and female college teachers: Part II—Evidence from students' evaluations of their classroom teachers. *Research in Higher Education, 34*, 151–211.

Finkelstein, M., & Schuster, J. (2001). Assessing the silent revolution: How changing demographics are reshaping the academic profession. *AAHE Bulletin of the American Association for Higher Education, 54*(2), 3–7.

Fisher, T. (2007, February 23). Roundtable discussion of campus architecture. *Chronicle of Higher Education*, pp. 38–39.

Freire, P. (2003). *Pedagogy of the oppressed* (M. B. Ramos, Trans.). New York: Continuum International. (Original work published 1971).

Gabelnick, F., MacGregor, J., Matthews, R., & Smith, B. L. (1990). *Learning communities: Creating connections among students, faculty and disciplines.* San Francisco: Jossey-Bass.

Gappa, J. M., Austin, A. E., & Trice, A. G. (2007). *Rethinking faculty work: Higher education's strategic imperative.* San Francisco: Jossey-Bass.

Gardner, H. (1983). *Frames of mind: The theory of multiple intelligences.* New York: Basic Books.

Gardner, H. (1999). *Intelligence reframed.* New York: Basic Books.

Gardner, J. W. (1990). *On leadership.* New York: Free Press.

Gergen, K. J. (1985). The social constructionist movement in modern psychology. *American Psychologist, 40*, 266–275.

Grasha, A. F. (1996). *Teaching with style: A practical guide to enhancing learning by understanding teaching and learning styles.* Pittsburgh: Alliance.

Greenleaf, R. K. (1977). *Servant leadership: A journey into the nature of legitimate power and greatness.* New York: Paulist Press.

Grunert, J. (1997). *The course syllabus: A learning-centered approach.* San Francisco: Jossey-Bass/Anker.

Guskin, A. E., & Marcy, M. B. (2002). Pressures for fundamental reform: Creating a viable academic future. In R. M. Diamond (Ed.), *Field guide to academic leadership* (pp. 3–15). San Francisco, CA: Jossey-Bass.

Hackman, R. J. (2002). *Leading teams: Setting the stage for great performances.* Boston, MA: Harvard Business School Press.

Hagedorn, L. S. (Ed.). (2000). *What contributes to job satisfaction among faculty and staff?* San Francisco: Jossey-Bass.

Haney, C., & Zimbardo, P. G. (1975). It's tough to tell a high school from a prison. *Psychology Today, (June)*, 26–36.

Harris, M., & Cullen, R. (2007). Learner-centered leadership: An agenda for action. *Innovative Higher Education, 33*(1), 21–28.

Harris, M., & Cullen, R. (2008a). Observing the learner-centered class. *Florida Journal of Educational Administration and Policy, 1*(1), 57–66.

Harris, M., & Cullen, R. (2008b). Supporting new scholars: A learner-centered approach to new faculty orientation. *Florida Journal of Educational Administration and Policy, 2*(1), 17+.

Harris, M., & Cullen, R. (2008c). Using assessment to bring about cultural change: The value of assessing learning spaces. *Assessment Update, 20*(3), 6–7, 10.

Hatfield, S. R. (Ed.). (1995). *The seven principles in action: Improving undergraduate education.* San Francisco: Jossey-Bass/Anker.

Heifetz, R. (1994). *Leadership without easy answers.* Cambridge, MA: Belknap Press.

Hennings, D. G. (1975). *Mastering classroom communication—What interaction analysis tells the teacher.* Pacific Palisades, CA: Goodyear.

Hersh, R., & Merrow, J. (Eds.). (2005). *Declining by degrees. Higher education at risk.* New York: Macmillan.

Hill, N. K. (1980, June 16). Scaling the heights: The teacher as mountaineer. *Chronicle of Higher Education*, 48.

Huber, M., & Hutchings, P. (2005). *The advancement of learning: Building the teaching commons.* San Francisco: Jossey-Bass.

Hunt, P. W., & Saul, P. N. (1975). The relationship of age, tenure, and job satisfaction in males and females. *The Academy of Management Journal, 18*(4), 690–702.

Jaschik, S. (2009, May 14). Students fail and professor loses job. *Inside Higher Ed*. Retrieved from http://www.insidehighered.com.

Jensen, E. (1995). *Brain-based learning*, San Diego, CA: Brain Store.

Johnsrud, J. K., & Rosser, V. J. (2002). Faculty members' morale and their intention to leave: A multilevel explanation. *The Journal of Higher Education, 73*(4), 518–542.

Jones, H. (2008, May 9). A student's view: Invest in people, not buildings. *Chronicle of Higher Education*, A30.

Jones, R. (1981). *Experiment at Evergreen*. Cambridge, MA: Shenkman.

Kalantizis, M., & Cope, B. (Eds.). (2002). *Transformations in language and learning: Perspectives on multiliteracies*. Melbourne, Australia, Common Ground.

Kerr, C. (1994). *Troubled times for American higher education: The 1990s and beyond*. Albany, NY: State University of New York Press.

King, A. (1993). From sage on the stage to guide on the side. *College Teaching, 41*(1), 3–4.

Kotter, J. P. (1996). *Leading change*. Boston: Harvard Business School Press.

Kouzes, J., & Posner, B. (2002). *The leadership challenge*. San Francisco: Jossey-Bass.

Kouzes, J., & Posner, B. (2003). *Academic administrator's guide to exemplary leadership*. San Francisco: Jossey-Bass.

Kuhn, T. (1962). *The structure of scientific revolutions*. Chicago: University of Chicago Press.

Langer, E. J. (1997). *The power of mindful learning*. Reading, MA: Addison-Wesley.

Leamnson, R. (1999). *Thinking about teaching and learning: Developing habits of learning with first-year college and university students*. Sterling, VA: Stylus.

Lederman, D. (2008, April 15). Margaret Spellings, where are you? *Inside Higher Ed*. Retrieved from http://www.insidehighered.com.

Lencioni, P. (2002). *The five dysfunctions of a team*. San Francisco: Jossey-Bass.

Lewis, H. (2006). *Excellence without a soul: How a great university forgot education*. New York: Public Affairs.

Lick, D. W. (2002). Leadership and change. In R. M. Diamond (Ed.), *Field guide to academic leadership* (pp. 27–47). San Francisco: Jossey-Bass.

Lucas, C. J. (1994). *American higher education: A history*. New York: St. Martin's.

MacTaggart, T. (Ed.). (2007). *Academic turnarounds: Restoring vitality to challenged American colleges and universities*. Westport, CT: Praeger.

Marton, F., & Booth, S. (1997). *Learning and awareness*. Mahwah, NJ: Erlbaum.

Marton, F., Hounsell, D., & Entwistle, N. (Eds.). (1977). *The experience of learning: Implications for teaching and studying in higher education* (2nd ed.). Edinburgh, Scotland: Scottish Academic Press.

Marton, F., & Saljo, R. (1976). On qualitative differences in learning: Outcome as a function of the learner's conception of the task. *British Journal of Educational Psychology, 46,* 115–127.

McKeachie, W. J. (1996). Student ratings of teaching. *American Council of Learned Societies Occasional Paper, No. 33.* Retrieved from http://archives.acls.org/op/33_Professional_Evaluation_of_Teaching.htm.

McKeachie, W. J., Lin, Y.-G., Daugherty, M., Moffett, M., Neigler, C., Nork, J., Walz, M., & Baldwin, R. (1980). Using student ratings and consultation to improve instruction. *British Journal of Educational Psychology, 50,* 168–174.

Meiklejohn, A. (1932). *The experimental college.* New York: Harper Collins.

Menges, R. J. (1999). Appraising and improving your teaching: Using students, peers, experts, and classroom research. In W. J. McKeachie, *Teaching Tips: Strategies, research and theory for college and university teachers.* Boston: Houghton Mifflin.

Menges, R. J., & Exum, W. H. (1983). Barriers to the progress of women and minority faculty. *Journal of Higher Education, 54*(2), 123–144.

Mezirow, J. (2000). *Learning as transformation: Critical perspectives on a theory in progress.* San Francisco: Jossey-Bass.

Millis, B. (2006). Peer observations as a catalyst for faculty development. In P. Seldin (Ed.), *Evaluating faculty performance: A practical guide to assessing teaching, research, and service* (pp. 82–96). San Francisco: Jossey-Bass.

Mintrom, M. (1997). Policy entrepreneurs and the diffusion of innovation. *American Journal of Political Science, 41,* 738–770.

Monroe, K., Ozyurt, S., Wrigley, T., & Alexander, A. (2008). Gender equality in academia: Bad news from the trenches and some possible solution. *Perspectives on Politics, 6,* 215–233.

Moody, J. (1997). *Demystifying the profession: Helping junior faculty succeed.* New Haven, CT: University of New Haven Press.

Murray, M. J., Rushton, J. P., & Paunonen, S. V. (1990). Teacher personality and student instructional ratings in six types of university courses. *Journal of Educational Psychology, 82,* 250–261.

Myron, G. (2008, May 5). Les miserables. *Demo Dirt.* Retrieved from http://www.demodirt.com/generation_x_miserable.html.

Near, J. P., Rice, R. W., & Hunt, R. G. (1978). Work and extra-work correlates of life and job satisfaction. *The Academy of Management Journal, 21*(2), 248–264.

Newman, F., Couturier, L., & Scurry, J. (2004). *The future of higher education: Rhetoric, reality and the risks of the market.* San Francisco: Jossey-Bass.

Nicholson, E. A., & Miljus, R. C. (1972, November). Job satisfaction and turnover among liberal arts college professors. *Personnel Journal,* 840–845.

Oblinger, D. (Ed.). (2000). *Learning spaces: An Educause e-book.* Retrieved from http://www.educause.edu/LearningSpaces/10569.

O'Brien, J. G., Millis, B. S., & Cohen, M. W. (2008). *The course syllabus: A learning-centered approach* (2nd ed.). San Francisco: Jossey-Bass.

Oshagbemi, T. (1997). Job satisfaction and dissatisfaction in higher education. *Education & Training, 39*(4), 354–359.

Parnell, D. (1988). Leadership is not tidy. *Leadership Abstracts, 4,* 1–2.

Peterson, M. (1997). Using contextual planning to transform institutions. In M. Peterson, D. Dill, L. A. Mets, & Associates (Eds.), *Planning and management for a changing environment* (pp. 127–157). San Francisco: Jossey-Bass.

Pielstick, C. D. (1997). The transforming leaders: A meta-ethnographic analysis. *Community College Review, 26*(3), 15–34.

Ramsden, P. (Ed.). (1988). *Improving learning: New perspectives.* London, England: Kogan Page.

Ramsden, P. (1992). *Learning to teach in higher education.* New York: Routledge.

Remmers, H. H. (1928). The relationship between students' marks and students' attitudes toward instructors. *School and Society, 28,* 759–760.

Rice, R. E., Sorcinelli, M. D., & Austin, A. E. (2000). *Heeding new voices: Academic careers for a new generation. New Pathways: Faculty Careers and Employment for the 21st Century Series* (Working Paper Inquiry No. 7). Washington, DC: American Association of Higher Education.

Russo, R. (1997). *Straightman.* New York: Random House.

Sabin, B. (2007). *Socialization of new college faculty: Mentoring and beyond.* Retrieved from http://www.brucesabin.com/socialization.html.

Schuster, J., & Finklestein, M. (2006). *The American faculty: The restructuring of academic work and careers.* Baltimore: Johns Hopkins University Press.

Seldin, P. (1993). The use and abuse of student ratings of professors. *Chronicle of Higher Education, 39*(46), A40.

Seldin, P. (2006). *Evaluating faculty performance: A practical guide to evaluating teaching, research, and service.* San Francisco: Jossey-Bass.

Seldin, P., & Higgerson, M. (2002). *The administrative portfolio: A practical guide to improved performance and personnel decisions.* San Francisco: Jossey-Bass/Anker.

Senge, P. (1990). *The fifth discipline: The art and practice of the learning organization.* New York: Doubleday.

Shapiro, N. S., & Levine, J. H. (1999). *Creating learning communities: A practical guide to winning support, organizing for change, and implementing programs.* San Francisco: Jossey-Bass.

Shulman, L. (2008). Stewards of change. *Change Magazine, 40*(3), 6–7.

Singham, M. (2005). Moving away from the authoritarian classroom. *Change Magazine, 37*(3), 50–58.

Smart, J. C. (1990). A causal model of faculty turnover intentions. *Research in Higher Education, 31*(5), 405–424.

Sommer, R. (1977). Classroom layout. *Theory into Practice, 16*(3), 174–175.

Sorcinelli, M., & Austin, A. (Eds.). (2000). *New directions for teaching and learning, No. 50. Developing new and junior faculty.* San Francisco: Jossey-Bass.

Spinks, N., Silburn, N., & Burchill, D. (2006). *Educating engineers for the 21st century: The industry view.* Oxfordshire, UK: The Royal Academy of Engineering.

Stage, F. K., Muller, P. A., Kinzie, J., & Simmons, A. (1998). *Creating learning-centered classrooms: What does learning theory have to say?* Washington, DC: The George Washington University.

Stevenson, H., & Stigler, J. (1992). *The learning gap: Why our schools are failing and what we can learn from Japanese and Chinese education.* New York: Simon & Schuster.

Sylwester, R. (1995). *A celebration of neurons: An educator's guide to the human brain.* Alexandria, VA: Association for Supervision and Curriculum Development.

Tagg, J. (2003). *The learning paradigm college.* San Francisco: Jossey-Bass/Anker.

Terenzini, P., & Pascarella, E. (1994). Living with myths: Undergraduate education in America. *Change, 26*(1), 28–32.

Thompson, J. (1973). *Beyond words: Nonverbal communication in the classroom.* New York: Citation Press.

Traversi, D. M. (2007). *The source of leadership: Eight drivers of the high impact leader.* Oakland, CA: New Harbinger.

Trower, C. A., & Bleak, J. L. (2002). *Harvard study of new scholars.* Retrieved from http://www.gse.harvard.edu/~newscholars/newscholars.

Turner, C., & Myers, L., Jr. (2000). *Faculty of color in academe: Bittersweet success.* Needham Heights, MA: Allyn & Bacon.

Vaill, P. (1996). *Learning as a way of being: Strategies for survival in a world of permanent whitewater.* San Francisco: Jossey-Bass.

Vest, C. (2007). *Educating engineers for 2020 and beyond.* Retrieved from http:mitworld.mit.edu.

von Glaserfeld, E. (1995). Constructivist approaches to science teaching. In L. P. Steffe & J. Gale (Eds.), *Constructivism in education* (pp. 3–15). Hillsdale, NJ: Erlbaum.

Vygotsky, L. (1978). *Mind and society: The development of higher mental processes.* Cambridge, MA: Harvard University Press.

Waldrop, M. (1996). The trillion-dollar vision of Dee Hock. *Fast Company, 5,* 75–81. Retrieved from http://www.fastcompany.com/learning.

Weimer, M. (2002). *Learner-centered teaching.* San Francisco: Jossey-Bass.

Weinstein, C. S., & Woolfolk, A. E. (1981). Classroom design and impression formation: A new area for research. *Contemporary Educational Psychology, 6,* 383–386.

White, E. K. (1990). Psychological aspects of classroom planning. *CEPPI's Educational Facility Planner, 28*(5), 4–6.

Williams, R., & Ory, J. D. (1992). *A further look at class size, discipline differences and student ratings.* Unpublished manuscript, Office of Instructional Resources, University of Illinois at Urbana-Champaign.

Wingspread Group on Higher Education. (1993). *An American imperative: Higher expectations for higher education.* Racine, WI: Johnson Foundation.

Zull, J. (2002). *The art of changing the brain: Enriching the practice of teaching by exploring the biology of learning.* Sterling, VA: Stylus.

Index